JUN 0 8 2006

D1298141

DSI:
DATE SCENE INVESTIGATION

ALSO BY IAN KERNER, PH.D.

She Comes First

He Comes Next

Be Honest—You're Not
That Into Him Either

DSI:

DATE SCENE INVESTIGATION

The Diagnostic Manual of Dating Disorders

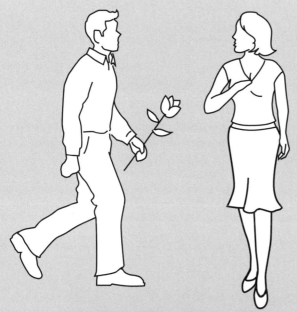

IAN KERNER, Ph.D.

ReganBooks
An Imprint of HarperCollins*Publishers*

HarperCollins books may be purchased for educational, business, or sales promotional use. For information please write: Special Markets Department, HarperCollins Publishers Inc., 10 East 53rd Street, New York, NY 10022.

FIRST EDITION

Designed by Kris Tobiassen

Printed on acid-free paper

Library of Congress Cataloging-in-Publication Data

Kerner, Ian.
    DSI—date scene investigation : the diagnostic manual of dating disorders / Ian Kerner.—1st ed.
        p. cm.
    ISBN: 0-06-088111-9 (alk. paper)
    1. Dating (Social customs)   2. Man-woman relationships.   3. Dating (Social customs)—Humor.   I. Title: Date scene investigation.   II. Title.

HQ801.K487 2006
306.73—dc22   2006042219

06 07 08 09 10 RRD 10 9 8 7 6 5 4 3 2 1

For Owen

MAY YOU GROW UP TO BE ONE OF THE GOOD GUYS

The names have been changed
to protect the brokenhearted.

CONTENTS:
OUTLINE OF CASE STUDIES

INTRODUCTION

Is your relationship an unsolved mystery?

Are you a victim of a crime of the heart?

Then it's time to review the relationship rap sheet, and analyze the Dating DNA!

Meet the DSI team, a rigorously trained clandestine unit within the FBI (that's the Federal Bureau of Intimacy), whose sole mission is to help everyday folks in everyday relationships figure out if it's time to dig in their heels or run for the hills.

Our handbook, *DSI—Date Scene Investigation: The Diagnostic Manual of Dating Disorders,* has been culled from years of top-secret investigative fieldwork and volumes of case studies that address some of today's most daunting dating dilemmas. Not for the faint of heart, this book tells of boyfriends who might be gay, gamers who won't step up to the plate, and wimps who won't *go down* for the count. You will see, first-hand, relationships ruined by bad timing, office politics, smoking, pornography, and marriage (to other people).

You will get to know heart-wrenching dating DUPEs (Desperately Under Pressure to Evaluate) and their antagonistic ARSEs (Anti-Relationship Suspect Examinees), and you will gain unprecedented access to previously classified relationship rap sheets: detailed reports that reveal interpersonal infractions, mating misdemeanors, and flirtatious felonies. You will be presented with in-depth psychographic portraits, which leave *all* laid bare.

Through the process of Relationship Reconnaissance, we will painstakingly reconstruct key Date Scene Investigations, including pivotal encounters subjected to rigorous Evidentiary Analysis. You will boldly go where no civilian has gone before as we apply the latest forensic tools to decipher complex dating data: from testing for SPARK (Sexual Potential And Romantic Kinship) to consulting with undercover agents in the MBU (Missing Boyfriends Unit), we take you with us as we venture above the law and beneath the covers.

Down the next block or over in the next cubicle or upstairs in your corner bedroom there lives Trouble: Someone you know is stuck in a dead-end relationship. Perhaps, that someone is even you.

The clues are all there, as elementary as Sherlock Holmes and his looking glass, just waiting to be detected. The fact that you're reading this suggests you're ready to shine the light of truth, well aware that the body you discover between the sheets may spell friend or end, groom or doom, stud or dud.

It's a tough job, but your courage will be well rewarded. Because in the end . . . ***the love life you save may be your own!***

ONE:

SHOULD HE STAY OR SHOULD HE GO?

THE CASE OF THE CAD WHO
COULDN'T COMMIT

THE DSI 911

At 11:22 P.M. on March 6, 2005, DSI received a frantic call from Dating DUPE (Desperately Under Pressure to Evaluate) Ms. Amelia Jacobs, who'd been dating her boyfriend for fourteen months. Things were going very well, and the relationship appeared to be heading in a positive direction. She believed it was moving toward the "next phase," and the ARSE (Anti-Relationship Suspect Examinee) gave clear indications that he was of a like mind and heart. Then, without warning, he began pulling away. Boundaries were imposed on the amount of time they should spend together. Other social and work obligations were introduced that precluded Friday night pizza and a movie. To cap it off, the suspect began reciting all of his faults and shortcomings, as if he were offering up ammunition to seal the deal with his own bullet. At her wit's end, the woman called DSI with the age-old question: was it time to cut bait? The DUPE felt that her boyfriend was acting in ways that were commitment-phobic, and she wanted to know if this situation could be saved.

PRELIMINARY DIAGNOSIS

Our preliminary diagnosis of the ARSE suggests he suffers from a Fear of Commitment Compounded by Underlying Pressures (aka FOCCed UP).

FOCCed UP is one of the most common forms of commitment phobias (others include "I'm Just Not Ready Syndrome" and "The It's Not You, It's Me Complex"). Its onset often comes as a surprise, since most suspects will hide their reservations until their fears become overwhelming and then make a run for it.

The causes of this phobia are many and varied, though, as is usually the case, it tends to take root in childhood, precipitated by a loss or trauma, such as parental separation, divorce, or bereavement. In some cases, a child who witnesses unhappily married parents or abusive interactions will grow up reluctant to form intimate relationships. To avoid the pain of possible rejection or loss, such persons will distance themselves, in an effort to remain in control.

PARALLEL CASE ANECDOTALS

A sampling of testimony from other recent DSI investigations reveals the following:

> "Monica was a lovely woman, and I really think that, had things been different, I might have asked her to marry me. But I was just at a different place in my life, and I wasn't ready to make the sacrifices that such a commitment required. I'm sure in the end it will turn out to be a stupid choice, but it was an honest one."
>
> **—Paul, 32**

"I realize that I'm very set in my ways and hard to please. And I'm trying to become more flexible, but I don't feel that I should compromise what is really important to me to make a relationship work. Things with Jane were great, but they were never at a level where I felt that she was the one, so I saw no reason for the relationship to continue."

—Mike, 35

"I was really surprised by the depth and intensity of the feelings that Jim expressed when I broke up with him. It was like a dam opened, and all of these emotions he'd walled off suddenly flooded out. It was sweet and lovely to learn that he cared so deeply for me, but it was too late. By the time he was able to communicate, I had already moved on."

—Margaret, 28

"Todd and I dated for three years, but throughout that time, we were really only together for two years. It seemed like we broke up for a month every six months, mostly because I grew tired of how passive he was. But then I'd dump him and he'd make such a strong effort to win me back, and I believed that each time was going to be for real. There was a certain intensity to the pattern, even though I knew it wasn't healthy. Eventually I had to break things off for good, no turning back."

—Summer, 33

CASE SPECIFICS

The Dupe: Amelia Jacobs
Age: 29
Location: New York, NY
Occupation: Fashion consultant
Hair: Brown
Eyes: Green
Height: 5'3"
Weight: 122

RELATIONSHIP RAP SHEET/EX FILES

Past Serious Relationships: 5
Total Number of Sexual Partners: 8
Exes Still in Contact: 3

Interpersonal Infractions

➤ Has a history of being a harsh judge of character, but is also exceptionally generous and giving

➤ Finds it difficult to maintain close friendships with other women because they get "too competitive"

➤ Her desire for a relationship is strengthened by the fact that both her older sisters are happily married with children

Mating Misdemeanors

August 1998

During her sophomore year of college, Ms. Jacobs constantly compared her boyfriend to her older sister's fiancé, and eventually broke things off because he didn't "measure up" in ways she felt were important in a potential husband, including professional achievement and financial solvency, which her boyfriend remonstrated was rather difficult at age nineteen. When he expressed shock that she was dissolving a perfectly happy relationship for not living up to her marital ideal before age twenty, Ms. Jacobs said, "I'll have plenty of time for fun once I'm married. Until then, I'm staying focused."

November 2000

Following a Valentine's Day dinner at The Olive Garden that wasn't as "romantic" as she had envisioned, accompanied by a second-tier box of chocolate by Lindt instead of Godiva, and a 14k gold-plated open heart necklace that was clearly a Paloma Picasso knockoff, Ms. Jacobs marched out of the restaurant and later withheld sex from her boyfriend for a week. Once he bought her a two-pound box of Godiva truffles and a genuine Tiffany 14k necklace, she made up for it by springing for a long weekend in a cabin in Vermont with a private outdoor hot tub, where they made love by candlelight in the middle of the night.

Flirtatious Felonies

February 2003

Broke off an engagement with her brother-in-law's boss, a man seventeen years her senior with two college-aged kids from a previous marriage, after he confessed he did not want to have more children. Ms. Jacobs was devastated, having endured two years of painstakingly dull sex accompanied by Frank Sinatra's greatest hits. After bringing up the subject of "cute nonbiblically derived girl names" for the thirteenth time in a month, her boyfriend finally folded his bluff. Ms. Jacobs was livid, nearly to the point of hurling her Cartier engagement ring, tennis bracelet, and tank watch in his face.

Psychographic Thumbnail

Ms. Jacobs is a complex character, driven by her desire to get married and start a family, yet unwilling to compromise on the ideals she prizes in a potential spouse. For most of her life she was the "prettiest girl in the room," and has rarely been alone. While she is not the type who needs a relationship to boost her self-confidence, she is accustomed to being the center of male attention. Nonetheless, her high standards limit the number of men she is willing to date. By her own admission, she often sells men short, cutting them loose at the first glimpse of something that doesn't match her exacting standards or mental profile.

As the youngest of three girls in a tight-knit family, she is the only one still single. Her two older sisters married soon after college and had children by the time they were thirty. But Ms. Jacobs is more ambitious than her siblings, and it was this desire that drove her to New York City to pursue a career in fashion. Having reached a comfortable plateau as a well-paid executive, she has set her sights on settling up this other piece of business and finding the right man to share her future.

Having recently broken off the engagement with the older man who had impeccable manners, flawless style, and a lovely backcountry estate in Greenwich, Ms. Jacobs is worried about "losing more precious time." She is singularly intent upon getting married, and is determined not to let anything stand in her way. To this end, she did not cancel her coveted reservation of the Wave Hill ballroom overlooking the Hudson River, scheduled for eighteen months hence, deciding she would never find a more ideal setting, and would sooner locate a new groom than miss out on the perfect wedding reception.

The Arse: Matthew Brown
Age: 33
Location: New York, NY
Occupation: Senior magazine editor
Hair: Brown
Eyes: Blue
Height: 6'
Weight: 170

RELATIONSHIP RAP SHEET/EX FILES

Past Serious Relationships: 6
Total Number of Sexual Partners: est. 45
Exes Still in Contact: 2

Interpersonal Infractions

→ Considered by friends to be a "perpetual bachelor," based on his checkered dating background, which has alternated between serious relationships and periods of promiscuity

→ Has a distinct inability to focus on the person he is with, and is often called out by dates for his "wandering eyes"

➤ His parents' divorce, when he was 14, has led him to be cynical of marriage and commitment in general

Mating Misdemeanors

October 1995

While living on a kibbutz in Israel, Mr. Brown broke up with a woman he'd been dating for six months. Spotting a "more attractive Israeli" while on a bike tour through Haifa one afternoon, he snuck off and fooled around with her in a nearby citrus grove during a lunch break. Then he spontaneously invited her to join the tour. Rather than tell the former girlfriend he wanted out, he simply made out with the new woman in front of her, figuring it would convey the same message. The ex-girlfriend exploded into tears and was seen peddling into the distance on her bike. By the time he and his new girlfriend returned from the trip, the ex-girlfriend had conveniently cleared out all her personal belongings from his apartment.

April 1998

The ARSE got involved with a married visiting scholar in his graduate writing program with the express understanding that the relationship would end upon her return to England. He told her that he only wished she weren't married, partly because it was an arcane institution, and partly because he felt "very strongly" for her. When she suggested that she would consider dissolving her troubled marriage to be with him, Mr. Brown realized he was not in love with her. He then changed his mind some hours after the plane took off, but decided it was already too late.

March 2001

Mr. Brown invited a woman he "fell madly in love with" during a ten-day hiking trip through the Canadian Rockies to come stay with him for as long as she wanted in his New York City studio on East 28th and Lexington. She took him up on his emphatic offer, but Mr. Brown subsequently announced at the airport receiving line that his feelings must have been the result of the dizzying altitudes, causing the woman severe depression and an early, unconsummated departure. He left a message on her home answering machine while he knew she was on the plane, saying: "I must have had a stomach bug. Please come back and stay for as long as you want." She never replied.

April 2002

After a whirlwind romance that began at a weekly Friends of Kosovo beer-drinking contest at the downtown Ear Inn, Mr. Brown decided that he had finally found true love. After three months of intense nonmonogamous dating ("because monogamy kills free will and desire," they agreed), the woman took the liberty of leaving a change of clothing and toothbrush in his apartment. The next night, while listening to Bob Dylan, she exclaimed, "I'm so tired of all those whiny white men. What a sniveling overrated stoner." Mr. Brown thereupon showed her to the door. Later, he regretted it, feeling he'd woefully overreacted. But he knew she would never take him back, because that was the kind of brilliant, passionate, utterly incredible woman she was.

Flirtatious Felonies

January 2002

After three years of on-and-off dating with his older girlfriend, a performance artist/social historian with a double graduate degree in anthropology and modern dance, Mr. Brown severed the relationship with a detailed letter, explaining how he "simply lack[ed] the creative inspiration to be with someone like her."

November 2004–August 2005

Mr. Brown engaged in a string of short, intense two- to three-week-long flings, ending each by saying that he "just got out of a tough relationship" and "needed some time alone."

Psychographic Thumbnail

Mr. Brown is, in the language of pop psychology, a "serial monogamist." This designation refers to a modern condition that most single women and men suffer from, to varying extents, leading them to pursue somewhat serious relationships until they find "the one," and terminating healthy relationships before they get *too* serious under the Hollywood-mediated assumption that "they'll know when it's right."

Raised in a communal collective in Greenwich Village by Liza (his birthing mother), Mitchell (his sperm donor/father), and various others who came and went as passion called, Mr. Brown grew up with an inveterate disdain for the "normative nuclear family structure." His loss of virginity with a poetess twice his age on his 16th birthday was cause for a potluck celebration. This was followed, a week later, by a farewell dinner, as said poetess decided it was time for her to chant elsewhere. Mr. Brown was devastated by the emotional blow, but forced himself to conceal his profound feelings of disappointment and loss after being told by Liza and Mitchell that such reactions were the result of mass market sentimentalism.

Even in his late thirties, Mr. Brown still displays certain tendencies that are more consistent with the post-collegiate years. The fact that he lives in a large city that provides a rich vein of available bedmates makes his lifestyle sustainable. The almost infinite sea of choices works against Mr. Brown, who is predisposed to doubt and indecision. While he believes he is simply a man living life to its fullest free from mainstream societal constraints, Mr. Brown's history reveals a pattern of deep regret once the relationships end. His MO is to remain passive and uncommitted until a partner voices discontent with the situation, at which point he happily joins her in berating his inability to commit until they reach a mutual decision for her to dump him. Once the relationship is over or soured, he safely expresses his "true feelings" of remorse and sadness. Of course, by this point it is generally too late, and his declarations are thus "safe" since they usually fall on deaf ears.

Despite the fact that it is his inaction that sabotages these relationships, the way they end allows him to play the romantic fool, sent tumbling by turbulent waves of love. While there is a certain amount of pain associated with these breakups and latent professions of love, Mr. Brown eventually recovers, only to begin the pattern anew.

RELATIONSHIP RECONNAISSANCE

The relationship between Ms. Jacobs and Mr. Brown had a storybook beginning. They met on an early fall evening—one of those glorious New York moments when everything seemed possible. Neither was "looking" for anything serious at the moment and both had come to the event (a short film series at the TriBeCa Film Festival) because they were fond of the short-documentary form. After a series of evocative showings, the group went to a rooftop cocktail party overlooking the Manhattan skyline. Ms. Jacobs spotted Mr. Brown and walked over to him. They talked until 2:00 that morning, then shared a plate of French fries at a bistro overlooking the river. Mr. Brown walked Ms. Jacobs to her SoHo studio and asked for her number and did not hesitate to call her the next morning. They went on their first date that weekend. From there the relationship blossomed, slowly at first, but in a manner that was consistent and unwavering. The first two months were more friendship than romance, and Mr. Brown showed every sign that he was emotionally ready for something real, while Ms. Jacobs tried to "play it cool."

At the six-month mark, Ms. Jacobs took Mr. Brown on a surprise trip to a yoga retreat in Tulum, Mexico, and she was pleased when he didn't wince at her desire to celebrate their "anniversary." While there were certain aspects about his past that Mr. Brown had kept private (his family and his past girlfriends, for example), Ms. Jacobs was very open and honest, and she believed he would "come around" in time, partially because Mr. Brown suggested as much. For the past two months they have been at the "same place," in a sort of limbo where they are not moving forward or backward. Ms. Jacobs has made her desires for a definite sense of direction clear, while Mr. Brown has only responded that he is "unsure" and he "needs time to think." This lack of passionate gusto has only made Ms. Jacobs more insistent on gleaning an answer from him: do they or do they not have a serious future together? While Mr. Brown is unable to answer that question, he is clear in his insistence that he is very much in love with Ms. Jacobs but "not sold on the whole idea of the marriage thing."

DATE SCENE RECONSTRUCTION

Five Months into Dating: A Crime of the Heart-burn

LOCALE: Ms. Jacob's bedroom

Synopsis: Following a romantic, home-cooked dinner five months into their relationship, Ms. Jacobs expressed her happiness with Mr. Brown and casually inquired "where their relationship was going." When the couple retired to the bedroom minutes later, Jacobs failed to initiate sexual intimacy, inconsistent with previous behavior. Assuming he hadn't heard her, Ms. Jacobs repeated her sentiment of happiness and innocently asked what he saw for their future, at which time Mr. Brown experienced a sudden bout of labored breathing, causing him to pull his head between his knees and pant like a febrile dog. Taking the question as a global inquiry into his intentions, he grew nervous (DSI reconstructive analysis revealed an increased heart rate and the onset of adrenaline, both of which occur during primal "fight or flight" situations). Ms. Jacobs later admitted that she was not necessarily looking for a long-term commitment or a guarantee with her question. Rather, she was simply seeking an expression of a reciprocated desire to move the relationship forward. Mr. Brown was unable to turn the romantic moment into an opportunity to discuss his reservations and feelings, and this further accelerated the internal spiral. The two ended up going to bed in angry silence, after Mr. Brown took a number of antacids to calm his gastrointestinal upset.

Witness Testimony: A clerk at a local deli observed Mr. Brown the next morning, buying flowers. When he jokingly asked what the occasion was,

Mr. Brown replied, "Nothing much, just making up for being myself again."

Seven Months into Dating: One Too Many Mornings

LOCALE: Mr. Brown's kitchen

Synopsis: During a weekend breakfast of bagels, lox, and fresh-cut fruit salad, Ms. Jacobs was reading the *New York Times* and perusing the wedding announcements. When she made a comment that one particular matrimonial story was "very sweet and touching," Mr. Brown grew agitated, opining that "all those couples are simply buying into the capitalist flotsam of individualism machinated to preempt the evolution of class consciousness." Ms. Jacobs was understandably taken aback, and the discussion turned to whether Mr. Brown, in fact, wanted to "get married in general." He again grew uneasy, responding with a sputter of guttural grunts. Thereupon, he launched into a heart-felt soliloquy on the subject of the "demise of the economic utility of the family unit in post-agricultural society and the concomitant derogation of women to chattel." Ms. Jacobs stomped out of the apartment, and did not return. Although Mr. Brown made no effort to stop her, he did apologize the next day, realizing it was "ideologically inscribed as the right thing to do."

Witness Testimony: Ms. Jacobs' doorman noticed she looked atypically teary and upset when she entered the building, which he found startling in such a "normally upbeat and attractive young lady."

One-year Anniversary: Out in the cold, Inn with a View

LOCALE: The Farmhouse Bed and Breakfast, Stowe, Vermont

Synopsis: While on a weekend ski trip coinciding with the couple's one-year anniversary of meeting, Mr. Brown seemed aloof and difficult at times despite the idyllic setting and the fact that Ms. Jacobs had planned and paid for the weekend as a special treat for the overworked Mr. Brown and had made a special trip to La Perla to "sweeten the pot." Upon seeing Ms. Jacobs splayed across the bed in a rather comely ensemble, Mr. Brown complained, "The bed is way too small for two people born in this century." When Ms. Jacobs pouted and said, "Are you sure you don't like the four-poster bed? If you'd like we can get another room," removing a set of pink feather handcuffs from her bag. He merely commented, "Oh, whatever, it's fine. All we're going to do is sleep here." He seemed not to notice the champagne she'd prearranged, and when she pointed out that it was the anniversary of the first day they met, he said, "It's not like we were screwing yet, so I hardly think it counts for much." She put it out of her head, assuming he was still stressed from work.

The next day, after an afternoon of skiing, they had a couple's massage and a dinner for two, during which Mr. Brown told Ms. Jacobs that he feared he had certain shortcomings with regard to his ability to "make her happy" and to "give her what she wanted." When she pressed him for details, he grew silent, vaguely referring to his "problems." They spent the rest of that evening and the following night battling uncomfortable silences and checked out a day early the next morning, despite the excellent snow conditions and Mr. Brown's former tenure as head of the socialist ski collective.

Witness Testimony: The hotel chambermaid noticed that only one side of the bed had been slept in, and the pullout couch had been in use. A ski patrolman who saw the couple on the slopes noted that Mr. Brown was making no effort to teach his partner, despite her clear status as a beginner.

FORENSIC ASSESSNENT AND EVIDENTIARY ANALYSIS

Physical Evidence

A DSI investigation of Mr. Brown's residence and office reveal findings consistent with a FOCCed UP condition, including:

→ While Ms. Jacobs gave Mr. Brown keys to her apartment, he did not reciprocate, his excuse being that he "rarely slept at his apartment."

→ Mr. Brown still maintains his "black book" and other mementos of his bachelor past.

→ Mr. Brown bought tickets for a scuba diving trip, knowing full well that Ms. Jacobs feared being underwater and would likely turn down the invitation.

→ Photographic evidence and ocular retinal-mapping suggests that Mr. Brown has a "wandering eye," indicative of a belief that there is someone out there better for him.

→ The presence of newly acquired condoms (Ms. Jacobs is on the pill), champagne, caviar, and romantic music suggests the possibility that Mr. Brown plans to entertain other women at his apartment, where Ms. Jacobs has yet to spend the night.*

Psychological Evidence

Because the nature of this particular disorder is as much about a state of mind as it is anything rooted in physical evidence and external actions, DSI has developed a forensic index that examines parallel behaviors consistent with one who is FOCCed UP, as a person's relationship persona is often consistent with personality traits in other areas of their life.

Work/Career: Mr. Brown's career as a senior (rather than managing) editor has been stalled by his inability to remain at one company for more than a year. While he defends his checkerboard resume as evidence of a gung-

---

DSI Note: While there is no evidence that Mr. Brown has been unfaithful at this time (a GPS [Genital Positioning Sweep] came back negative), DSI's determination was that the presence of these totems of singlehood were maintained as a means of creating the illusion that he was still "free" and, as such, they are indicative of a bachelor lifestyle and patent disinclination to commit.

ho, in-and-up-or-out attitude, consistent with the fast-track magazine trade, his employers suggest he "grows bored easily" and is addicted to the "honeymoon period" a new job engenders, easily growing restless once he masters the challenges, remarking that something better is probably around the next corner. Mr. Brown seems unable to lay down roots, and he is thus considered something of a journeyman.

Friendships: While Mr. Brown has many old and deep friendships, many of these suffer from a lack of actual physical interaction. With email and instant messaging, Mr. Brown is able to maintain these relationships in a way that makes them real, without requiring actual contact. As previously stated, Mr. Brown has been described by such friends as rootless, with a tendency to go long periods of time incommunicado interspersed by random intervals of intense contact.

Family: Mr. Brown's family life is both rich and full of turbulence. His parents both still live in the communal West Village collective where he was raised, but both are involved with other people. Mr. Brown has two brothers and a sister, all of whom were granted liberal license to go and come as they please and given generous allowances without need for explaining expenditures from an early age. While the family maintains a sense of convivial comfort and a closeness during "key moments" (potluck dinners and solstice banquets), there is no larger sense of loyalty or connectedness. Mr. Brown floats in and out of the lives of his family members as time and desire permit.

Housing/Life Plans: Despite a sizable trust fund inherited from an unremembered paternal aunt, Mr. Brown has not purchased an apartment in Manhattan, preferring to remain in a run-down illegal airshaft sublet in an overpriced fifth-floor walk-up in Murray Hill until he decides where he wants to "settle down." Mr. Brown often fixates on relocating to various points across the country, such as Juno, Alaska; Ashland, Oregon; and Santa Fe, New Mexico (none of which he has ever visited), after he procures a red Chevy pickup, a Dalmatian named Dutchess (although he is allergic to dogs), and a driver's license, whereupon he will finish penning his first literary novel, a dark comedic tragedy of 120,000 words, of which he has thus far typed a whopping 5,728.

Forensic Metrics

Commitment-Repellant Assessment Placement (CRAP) Test

The advanced form of CRAP pinpoints the relative degree of an ARSE's inability to commit (and comes into play only after a primary evaluation meets a steep threshold of CRAP). Results are based on a variety of oral, behavioral, and psychographic factors, including body language and physical response to emotional stimuli, leading to a final determination ranging from "not to worry" to "hang in baby" to "hide the Häagen-Dazs"). In Mr. Brown's case, the CRAP test found him a "serious waffler," with a high countervailing measure of self-awareness, and a core desire to overcome his phobia. Such result is not necessarily indicative of a favorable outcome, but rather points to a borderline situation, requiring advanced clinical treatment.

Body and Oral Language Test (BOLT)

An examination of Mr. Brown's body language and voice patterns over a variety of situations (with and without Ms. Jacobs, and also with Ms. Jacobs during moments when she is asking about the future versus those moments where the conversation is more general) revealed a heightened level of fear during periods of confrontation. From this, DSI determined that Mr. Brown's phobia has physical manifestations, including heart palpitations and gastrointestinal distress. Moreover, the BOLT analysis compares an ARSE's gesture/voice patterns to thousands of others to determine attitude and emotions. Mr. Brown's BOLT readings fell well outside the median normal readings.

Sexual Arousal Signal Sampling (SASS) Analysis

DSI utilized a SASS test to determine the level of sexual chemistry between Ms. Jacobs and Mr. Brown. Often, an inability to commit can be triggered by "sexual boredom" or a lack of connection in this area. However, Mr. Brown's reaction to SASS was fairly high, and hence sexual dysfunction was concluded irrelevant to the current case [the results revealed an adequate level of HEAT (Highly Erotic Attractiveness Traces), so it was determined that the root cause of Mr. Brown's noncommittal issues were not sexually related].

DSI FINDING

Mr. Brown has a strong to severe case of commitment phobia, marked by many of the classic hallmarks. While the roots of this phobia may not be his fault (i.e., most are linked to unresolved childhood issues), that is no excuse for his failure to undertake an appropriate course of remedial therapy. Mr. Brown seems to have a deep fondness for Ms. Jacobs and a genuine awareness and desire for recovery. For this reason, this case has been forwarded to the Relationship Rehab unit for continued monitoring, treatment, and intervention consistent with this finding.

RELATIONSHIP REHAB

Given our finding that Mr. Brown is a self-aware "waffler" with a genuine desire, however conflicted, to achieve lasting intimacy with Ms. Jacobs, DSI recommends:

→ A short probationary period followed by an extended course of individual therapy.

→ Mr. Brown must begin to tap his inner adult and show a more refined level of maturity and, more important, an ability to recognize the early symptoms of a commitment-phobic episode (i.e., inference of lasting togetherness followed by intervals of heavy breathing, desire to flee, and panic-driven expulsions of intellectual hyperbole or sullen silence).

→ Once Mr. Brown is able to identify the danger signs, the couple can begin to work through these difficult moments together.

➤ Ms. Jacobs is advised to cancel her wedding hall reservation, and focus on the quality of her interactions with Mr. Brown, without regard for her external desires to marry.

➤ Ms. Jacobs must learn to enjoy the moment without placing so much pressure on how each moment connects to her "big picture" goals.

DATING DIAGNOSTIC

Those of us who've been through the rinse cycle a few too many times sometimes run before we're ready to walk. When the going gets tough, we bolt. It's an irresistible impulse we may indulge now and regret later. We pretend we'll fix the problem when the moment demands it. But by the time that moment comes, we're generally miles from the closed door.

As a culture weaned on the concept of "true love," we cling to the myth of Mr. and Ms. Right, waiting for "true love" to bonk us on the heads and announce itself, before we give it our full attention. Until that time, we focus on other things like our careers and our social lives, we date and dabble, figuring that when that special person comes along, we'll know it and spring into action. The problem is we don't have realistic perceptions of what "true love" looks like beyond the heat of early romance. As a result, we fail to appreciate the relationships we're in. When ordinary life intercedes and the sizzle chills, we bolt, assuming that if this *were* the right person, we'd be more committed to working it out. We're not going to settle for second best and get trapped in unsatisfying relationships, like most of our parents and friends. We expect better, so we'll sit this dance out. It's an odd tautology, and one that is difficult to escape: if we really loved so-and-so, we'd *want* to work it out. But the truth is, if we tried to work it out with so-and-so, we might discover we truly loved him or her, before it was too late.

Hey, it's natural to get a little queasy once things start to get serious. Even when we're head over kneecaps in love, there is something about the word *forever* that induces dry heaves and cold sweats. Forever! Say it: Forever. Yeah, it hurts.

Now some of us mature types realize that this sort of anxiety is inevitable. We know it's not about the poor schlub we happen to be dating, it's about the possibility of committing ourselves to one person, and only one person, forever. Forever. (Breathe—and swallow.) Sure, they're great. We're darn lucky to have them in our beds and we understand that hot passion can grow over time with sufficient effort, honesty, and a sense of adventure. But all the same, we have limited attention spans. We've been culturally programmed to crave sexual novelty, variety, and to shop 'til we drop (it's not our fault, society is to blame)! Yes, we like our partners. Hell, maybe we even *Love* our partners. But to never enjoy another first kiss or hot squeeze or fondle or grope (maybe two) or lick (maybe seven) . . . *Forever*?? Yeah, still hurts.

Yet sometimes we know, deep down, that even though it makes us want to puke up yesterday's lunch, the thought of *not* waking up next to so-and-so twenty years from now is *not* a risk we're willing to take. After all, we want to set up college funds for our kids together and build a doghouse in our backyards and go to early bird dinners and argue about whether it's time to go for our annual teeth cleanings. Why? Because, the truth is, we'd rather fantasize about a first kiss and be with him or her than enjoy a first kiss with anyone else.

So the next time you get that jittery crackle in your bones while discussing "where the relationship is headed," close your eyes and take a deep breath. Imagine it's ten years from now. Is that person still sitting across from you? Do you want him or her to be? If the answer is yes, say so. Then pitch off your tomorrow blinders and revel in the moment you're in.

FOLLOW-UP

A one-year follow-up showed Ms. Jacobs and Mr. Brown cohabitating in domestic bliss, with the bouts of commitment-phobic anxiety having all but disappeared. Further DSI investigation revealed that Mr. Brown had purchased a "near-perfect" engagement ring several months earlier, but had yet to propose in the quest to formulate the ideal setting for popping the question, to which end he had consulted the producers of the

TriBeCa Film Festival and commissioned a short documentary film showing him on bended knee, to be shown on the eve of their next anniversary (which he no longer disputed as the precise moment he first laid eyes on Ms. Jacobs). Consistent with Mr. Brown's general reservations about the productization of marriage, Ms. Jacobs has come to terms with the possibility of eloping and enjoying a potluck dinner in the garden of the "family" collective.

IS COMMITMENT PHOBIA UNDERMINING YOUR RELATIONSHIP?

Are either or both of you guilty of any of the following?

1. Being overly critical of the other partner regarding his or her suitability as a mate and/or of the relationship as a whole.

2. Deliberately offending or creating contention, thus sabotaging the relationship, even if seems to be working well. An example of this might be consistently showing up late for dates, being passive during situations that call for emotional action, or bringing up subjects in which there is known disagreement or discord.

3. Assuming a deer-in-the-headlights look of terror if one of you mentions "how great things are going" or "how perfect you are for each other."

4. Maintaining an overwhelming preoccupation with the concept that *true* love, or basically anything, is supposed to last "forever."

5. Experiencing anxieties or premonitions of failing at the relationship due to experiences as a child.

6. Fearing of loss of freedom or autonomy, and a sense of losing a separate identity distinct from the relationship.

7. Experiencing inability to calmly discuss the possibility of living together or getting married after several months of monogamous dating.

8. Levying global indictments of marriage, family, and/or the concept of finding the perfect mate, i.e., "there is no such thing as happily married"; "Everybody gets divorced"; "Women are sexy until you put that ring on their finger."

9. Falling for partners who are unavailable, married, live a long distance away, or have similar reservations about commitment.

10. Manifesting other forms of commitment-phobia, such as an ongoing inability to remain at jobs or at the same residence or even maintain long-term friendships (sometimes described as rootlessness).

DSI MOST WANTED FUGITIVE

WANTED FOR:

RECKLESS DISREGARD FOR HIS OWN TACKINESS; OVERUSE OF SYNTHETIC FABRICS AND HAIR PRODUCTS; DELUSIONS OF HIS OWN ROMANTIC GRANDEUR; LOOKING AT OTHER WOMEN IN THE PRESENCE OF A GIRLFRIEND WITH NO ATTEMPT TO CONCEAL HIS ACTION

Mick Slagger

Aliases: Slick Mick; Mikey Likey; Lover Toy; Eat 'em and Weep, DREAMBOY (this name adorns the vanity license plate of his late-model Corvette as well)

DESCRIPTION

Date of Birth: 1965

Place of Birth: Cleveland, OH

Height: 5' 11"

Weight: Approximately 160

Build: Moderate

Hair: Brown

Eyes: Brown

Complexion: Olive

Sex: Male

Nationality: American

Occupation: Unknown, though witnesses have heard him speak of his "day trading" successes; others have referred to him as a "small-time club promoter"

Remarks: Slagger is a well-known Lothario who hangs out with his high school buddies in less than savory clubs, where he attends various promotional activities (mainly wet t-shirt contests). He has two ex-wives, both of whom he wooed with breast augmentations and time-shares in Cancun. He is often seen with women who appear under the age of 25; Slagger relies on a brief to extended period of seduction in which he professes his love and ownership of a sports car that is, in fact, registered to his elderly mother.

Scars and Marks: Barbwire tattoo around his right bicep; earring in his left ear; all-season, all-body tan; wears tinted D&G sunglasses indoors

CAUTION

MICK (THE HICK) SLAGGER IS WANTED IN CONNECTION WITH NUMEROUS COUNTS OF LAME-ASS BEHAVIOR, INCLUDING THE PURCHASE OF A RED SPORTS CAR FOR HIS 40TH BIRTHDAY AND THE PRESENCE OF A STEVEN SEAGAL-LIKE PONYTAIL AFTER THE YEAR 1997. HE IS A DSI MOST WANTED FUGITIVE BECAUSE HE HAS THUS FAR BEEN SUCCESSFUL AT WOOING WOMEN WITH THE AID OF BOOZE, PERSISTENCE, AND FALSE FLATTERY ONLY TO DUMP THEM AFTER A BRIEF BUT INTENSE COURTSHIP ENDING IN UNGRATIFYING SEX OF UNKNOWN ORIGIN. HE HAS NO RESERVATION IN USING THE "L" WORD OR TALKING ABOUT WANTING KIDS AND MARRIAGE TO "GET A BABE BETWEEN THE SHEETS."

THIS INDIVIDUAL IS CONSIDERED CHEESY, SLIMY, AND EXTREMELY DANGEROUS TO ONE'S ROMANTIC STATE OF MIND; HE SHOULD BE DATED ONLY WITH EXTREME CAUTION.

IF YOU HAVE ANY INFORMATION CONCERNING THIS PERSON, PLEASE CONTACT YOUR LOCAL DSI OFFICE IMMEDIATELY

REWARD

The Rewards for Romance Gone Awry Program is offering a reward of up to $100,000 for information leading directly to the apprehension or conviction of MICK SLAGGER. An additional $50,000 is being offered through a program codeveloped and jointly funded by the Women Against Drunk Jivers and the America Drakar Noir Abuse Association.

TWO:

THE HONEYMOON IS OVER

THE CASE OF THE GUY WHO
GOT COMFY TOO QUICKLY

Given the overwhelming number of 911 calls DSI has received regarding this particular crime-of-the-heart, we present herewith testimony from *three* different ARSEs and the DUPEs who love[d] them.

CASE ONE: THE MAN WITH THE DIRTY SOCKS

Paul and Anna have been dating for five months since meeting through an online dating service. Things progressed very quickly, and while Paul was extremely fastidious during the first months of courtship, Anna has expressed dismay over his recent slip into sloppiness, telling friends he needs additional "toilet training" with reference to his tendencies to leave the seat up, the towels wet, the water dripping, the floor dirty, the dispenser empty, and the air foul.

ANNA'S TESTIMONY

"When we first met, Paul was so sweet and clean cut. In fact, his neat demeanor was one of the things that first attracted me to him. I just loved the way he dressed, and his attention to detail seemed evident even in the way that he treated me, if that makes any sense at all. In my past relationships, I dated guys who didn't pay much attention to what I liked. But Paul made me feel like I was the center of his world. When we would spend the night at his apartment, he would scrub the toilet, make the bed, and make sure everything was absolutely perfect—candles, flowers, bedding—he even got me Kiehl's face cream and eucalyptus toothpaste. It was so touching.

"But soon after the three-month point, something changed. Instead of flowers and candles, I'd get invited back to a smelly apartment to watch a pay-per-view sports event. He slowly reverted back to the slob he clearly was to begin with. I couldn't help feeling like he just didn't care about me anymore. I considered bringing it up, since he knew from my online profile that I was a 'compulsive tidier,' but I was afraid I'd come off like a nag (my last boyfriend accidentally called me 'Mom' one day when I was down on my knees scrubbing his toilet, which was sort of a wake-up call).

"I think the final straw came I was getting out my laptop at work one day for an important PowerPoint presentation and one of his stinky socks came tumbling out of my Tumi briefcase. For the life of me, I can't imagine how he managed to kick it so far across the room that it wound up in there, but, well, that was pretty much it for me.

"After that, whenever Paul bounded through the door straight from a pick-up game, hurling his sweaty clothing any old place and hoisting his foul body onto my pristine chenille sofa, I felt myself cringe from my pinkie toes to my eyelashes. If he reached over to kiss me, I instinctively pulled away. It wasn't intentional or anything. He was just . . . well, so disgusting. All I could do was wonder what had happened to that polished prince I'd met several months ago and who, in Satan's name, was this malodorous beast that had swallowed him up?

"Growing up I'd always dreamed of finding a handsome, well-dressed prince, one who would take me away from all my messy problems. Paul was that prince, at least for a little while, but then he went and turned back into a frog."

PAUL'S TESTIMONY

"I've always been a well dressed guy. I'm not ashamed to admit it: I follow fashion. But it extends beyond fashion, and includes art and architecture, and stuff like that. When I took Anna out for the first time to a downtown gallery opening, well, honestly, I was blown away. Everything about her screamed class, originality, and style. Most women are slaves to what other folks call trendy, but Anna seemed to go her own way. I was smitten. I figured the only way I was going to get this girl was to blaze my own trail in terms of style. So, in a way, she inspired me to become a better dresser, and to take more pride in my apartment, too. I really spruced up the place. I got rid of my black leather couch and my old college milk crates filled with papers and CDs and back issues of *Maxim* magazine.

"And it seemed to work. She loved spending time at my apartment, and she was forever complimenting my sense of style. I loved dressing up, and I didn't mind having to keep my home neat and tidy either. As I told her myself, she inspired me to reach and made me a better person. But, I'm still a guy, you know? And a certain level of just being my messy old self is necessary.

"But when I became more relaxed in some of my habits, Anna became agitated. She seemed to take it as a reflection of my feelings for her, which it was, but in a different way than she thought. I guess I trusted her enough to think she'd like me regardless of how I was dressed or if I didn't clean the bathroom three times a week. I felt like I could just be myself with her, and that she would accept me for who I am. To me, that guy is not such a bad person. That's what I thought mature relationships were supposed to be about. I was simply being me. But somehow she took it as an affront, based on what I was like the first few months.

"But hey man, this is who I am. I'm a man. My socks smell when I play ball. And sometimes I sweat just because. I just don't understand why it's such a big deal. To me the fact that I am comfortable enough to lie around in my boxers watching football is an indication of just how well things are going. But apparently . . . *not*."

DSI ASSESSMENT

In the case of Paul and Anna, DSI investigations determined that even though the Sock Odor Undesirable Reading (SOUR) in Paul's apartment was off the charts ("rank" was the reading), theirs was a situation that could be salvaged. Paul was indeed justified in believing that his level of comfort was indicative of deeper feelings for Anna. In any relationship, some level of give and take must be tolerated if the relationship is going to succeed. Anna harbored some unreasonable fantasies that no man could live up to, based on her romanticized Barbie-doll notions of the ideal boyfriend. Anna had gotten a taste of the Malibu dream house and didn't want to let go. Meanwhile, Paul did become "lax with the slacks." Though he had the financial resources he lacked the emotional wisdom to hire someone to come in and clean his apartment once or twice a month, if all else failed. The good news is the situation is not irreversible. Neither Anna nor Paul has violated any cardinal rule. They just have to try a little harder to understand each other's needs and limitations. Whether it comes to squeezing the toothpaste from the bottom, neglecting to align the pillows on the bed just so, or leaving dirty dishes in the sink ("even though the dishwasher is like six inches away" according to Anna), if a couple is going to make it over the long haul, they have to overcome the basic challenges of tolerating each other's daily routines. Negotiating these superficial differences rarely presents a fatal roadblock. In the current situation, it's just small change, as it were.

RELATIONSHIP REHAB

→ Paul needs to hire someone to clean the apartment twice a week and buy new socks.

➤ Anna needs to stop comparing Paul to some illusory ideal and appreciate him for who he is, instead of trying to convert him to who she wants him to be.

➤ Paul needs to make an effort to recapture the sense of inspiration, and aspiration, he felt in the early days of his relationship with Anna.

➤ Anna needs to appreciate, or at least tolerate, the many facets that comprise Paul's identity.

DATING DIAGNOSTIC

Women and men focus on visuals in different, often competing, ways. While women frequently condemn men for forming attractions to potential mates based on first, visually cued impressions, women are, in fact, just as prone to factor aesthetics into evaluating the viability of a long-term partner. To put it more bluntly, a man could spot a gorgeous girl sitting in the center of a garbage dump and fall instantly in love without bothering to inquire how she got there, whereas a woman is more likely to extrapolate opinions about the man based on his surroundings. A messy apartment, less-than-stellar hygiene, a shabby hole-in-the-wall restaurant, and/or a cheap motel, can all put a woman out of the mood. Not necessarily so with a man. This can lead to a lot of confusion, hurt feelings, and disappointment on both sides. A woman may read a man's lack of attention to detail as a romantic slap in the face, while a man may consider the woman's diminished attraction a personal rejection, rather than a response to an unsavory setting. The answer is learning to compromise on issues you may not understand, but still must do your best to accept.

FOLLOW-UP

A six-month follow-up found Paul and Anna looking for a duplex apartment with two separate bathrooms and a hermetically sealed sock drawer.

CASE TWO: WELCOME TO THE GRAND ILLUSION

Marco and Patricia have been dating for four months. Thanks to Marco's high-profile job and high-speed connections, it's been a whirlwind of movie premieres, black-tie events, and long weekends on Martha's Vineyard. Patricia was literally swept off her feet—wined and dined until her friends winced with envy. And while she was not the type to "demand" this sort of treatment from a boyfriend, she didn't exactly complain at the lavish attention and extravagant lifestyle. But then Marco started pulling back, at first a little, and then a lot. The champagne and caviar turned to wine and cheese and then to coffee and crullers and, now, leftover Chinese takeout. Patricia is a bit confused by Marco's sudden behavioral shift. And while she really enjoys spending time with him (and cuddling together), she's worried that his feelings for her have waned.

PATRICIA'S TESTIMONY

"When I first met Marco, I really wasn't that interested in him, or anyone else for that matter. I had just broken up with someone, so I was focusing on my new curatorial position at the Gardner Museum in Boston as well as preparing to defend my dissertation in art history. But it was like magic. Marco and I smiled at each other over Monet's *Floribunda*. And from that afternoon on, he started bringing me fresh flowers every day, for two whole weeks. They started calling me "Ms. Tulips" around the museum. Eventually, I agreed to go out with him. My intuition was telling me one thing, but he was so charming, that I just couldn't help myself.

"From there he began an old-fashioned courtship. I was raised in a traditional family, and while some of his efforts were corny, I loved his romantic gestures. He was unlike any other man I'd ever dated (the rest seemed to believe a couple of vodka tonics could transform an educated, professional woman into a slobbering sex slave). But Marco was different. His goodnight kisses were succinct, yet indicative of deeper passions. And that seemed like a very good sign.

"Over the first couple of months, it was like we were in a nineteenth-century novel or something. I'd come to work and find cards, or quirky gifts, or puzzles, telling me to meet him at a certain place, and he'd have a balloon ride or a romantic dinner on a sailboat planned. I never knew what to expect. He was winning my heart over just by being a gentleman. My girlfriends couldn't believe the stories I told them. Some were even skeptical, although I thought it was just plain envy. All I knew was I was falling hard and fast.

"The first time we made love was during a long surprise weekend in Montreal. We arrived and stayed in a charming hotel in the old part of the city. Marco grew up in Europe and his French was excellent. I was so impressed that I literally begged him to take me on the large four-poster bed in our room, and we didn't leave the hotel for the rest of the trip.

"It was after that weekend that I noticed a subtle change in his behavior, and it was only because he had set such a high bar to begin with that it was even discernible. The gentlemanly gestures that had once been a daily occurrence began to dwindle, and I was no longer the sole focus of his attention. Work seemed to intercede more and more, to the extent that he began missing our daily lunch meetings or canceling dates altogether. When we did see each other, he often cobbled something together at the last minute.

"We have now reached a point where I feel like he is taking me for granted, now that he's already 'had' me. In a way, I feel as though I was a conquest he won with grandiose gestures, that requires minimal upkeep. He claims it's simply a matter of bad timing, that he's stressed out at work, and that he wants to get back to the romance of the beginning. For me, it has less to do with the material totems than it does his momentous drop in attentiveness. I just don't feel like a priority anymore.

MARCO'S TESTIMONY

"The first time I saw Patricia I felt as though I was looking at a living Botticelli painting. She was so enigmatic and beautiful, so evanescent and full of light, like a living piece of art. I was raised in Europe, so perhaps my view of courtship is more established, but I treated her like a priceless treasure, placing her on a pedestal from the first time we met. Perhaps this was a mistake, as it set her expectations too high, but I did not know how else to act. Like Shakespeare's Romeo, I longed to be a glove on Patricia's hand in order that I might be able to touch her cheek.

"From the beginning I lavished her with gifts and attention, though it was not an act, or any sort of effort. This was simply what I felt she deserved. She far outshined any of the girls I'd dated recently, with whom I grew bored after a few weeks of sex. But there was something different about Patricia. And I wanted to preserve that purity for as long as possible.

"And, while it might seem like my acts of kindness were somehow wonderful or selfless, I derived great pleasure from making her so happy, so, in a way, there was a selfish joy to giving. Every flower, every note card, every trip we took to the sea was a chance for me to bask in her glow, and that made me feel good. She seemed so delighted and enamored, which made it easy to keep them going.

"After the heartache of the break-up with my last girlfriend, for whom everything was never enough, it was exhilarating to be with a woman who appreciated every little thing I did. She kept ticket stubs and took photos, and she made scrapbooks. When I would order a bottle of wine, she'd keep the cork. She enjoyed everything I gave her, and I loved that sense of power to make her happy.

"Eventually, however, I felt that she was becoming frustrated about my lack of physical attention. I was very attracted to her, but the notion of waiting seemed nice. Still, I felt she might begin to think I was not interested or manly enough, so I felt something had to be done. I made arrangements to go to Montreal for the weekend. It was the closest thing to Paris I could think of, and it certainly set the mood. We had a lovely time, and everything felt natural and right."

"I felt we'd reached a new point in the relationship after that trip. We were spending more time together, and I felt the courtship period was over. While Patricia may complain that my behavior has changed, my level of appreciation has not diminished one iota. This has been coupled with a busy stretch at work, which has left less free time to make plans and get together. But this is a temporary situation, and I find it hard to believe she is not more understanding of what a stressful period I'm going through, especially after all those months I spent wooing her.

"If anything, the fact that we've shifted out of the courtship mode and into the couple mode is evidence of how right we are together. I trust what we have established enough to be able to kick back a little. She should be looking at this as a positive sign of my comfort level, not a negative lack of attentiveness."

DSI ASSESSMENT

Patricia and Marco are going through what seems to be a very normal post-honeymoon phase, which typically occurs at the three- to six-month mark of a relationship, when the days of wine and roses are replaced by hectic schedules and take-out dinners. This is not a relationship-ending situation, depending on how a couple deals with it. In this case, however, DSI has also detected the symptoms of a "madonna-whore" complex. Marco appears to place women into one of two categories, and then tempers his behavior accordingly. Patricia was, for the duration of the courtship, placed in the "pure" devotion camp, and, as such, Marco paid appropriate homage to preserve her honor. But from the moment they became sexual, his behavior changed. It was not that he achieved his conquest and grew bored. Rather, in his eyes, Patricia no longer warranted adoration.

RELATIONSHIP REHAB

→ Marco has to be honest with himself and Patricia about his deep-seated views of women and marriage and whether he is willing/able to disabuse himself of his long-held, outdated convictions.

→ Patricia has to decide if she can live with the fact that she will never be regarded in the same pristine light as when they first fell in love.

DATING DIAGNOSTIC

This is a tricky case. In spite of Marco's clearly strong feelings for Patricia, it is unlikely she will ever recapture the exultant rush of their early courtship. While it is understandable that Marco is going through a difficult phase at work, Patricia was correct in apprehending a demonstrable change in his underlying attitude. Although Marco could turn out to be a loyal husband and devoted father, she will never again be a chaste paragon of perfection in his eyes. And that might not sit well with a progressive American woman. Perhaps love and effort will help Marco realize that Patricia is the same beautiful woman he first treasured beyond all else, or perhaps Patricia will instead seek out a partner who may not deify her as an angel, but will not devalue her as common for being a sexually active woman. DSI recommends further investigation with respect to just how "old-fashioned" her European-born beau is before Patricia finds herself in the chastened shrine of a Madonna, hailed for her selfless maternal devotion to the exclusion of all else (including pleasure-driven passion)!

FOLLOW-UP

A six-month follow-up found Marco and Patricia incommunicado. Marco grew angry with Patricia's demands for attention, saying a woman should gratefully receive, but never expect, lavish treatment. Patricia decided that she'd rather put her passion into French Impressionism than into Italian chauvinism.

CASE THREE: THANK-YOU FOR NOT SMOKING

Jason and Connie have been together for about seven months. They met at work and were friends for about a year before they began dating. Their initial interactions were in front of the office building, where they were part of a small, tight-knit band of cigarette smokers banished to the sidewalks. Connie quit smoking shortly after getting laid off and has not smoked since. Jason quit as well, although he recently resumed. This issue has become a divisive thorn in the side of their relationship.

CONNIE'S TESTIMONY

"Jason and I were friends for a while before we started dating, but we didn't know each other very well. He was a workplace acquaintance who blossomed into something more once I left the company. I guess we were both interested, but we thought it was a bad idea to mix business and pleasure.

"After I was laid off, we kept in touch, mostly using instant messenger and exchanging office gossip. Eventually he got up the nerve to ask me out, and it kind of went from there. Things started off slow, but given our history, I felt very secure with him. He was not some random guy I had met on a blind date or using an Internet dating service. We had a history and knew lots of the same people, and it gave us a common frame of reference and a foundation.

"Jason seemed to really appreciate having me as a girlfriend, after treading water in the dating pool for a long time. I remember listening to him complain when we used to hang out and smoke together how he just wanted to meet a nice girl who would appreciate him. Well, he found one: me.

"One of the main bonds we had was that we were both reformed smokers. This was a strong and constructive aspect of our relationship, since we helped each other remain smoke-free. I had been smoking since college, and getting off nicotine was hard for me. But when my grandmother passed away from lung cancer, I made a promise to myself. I was thirty-one, and I wanted to have children, so I wanted to be as healthy as possible.

"Jason had had an equally hard time quitting and staying away from cigarettes. I felt good about being able to help him through the struggle. To me it was imperative that I not date a smoker, for obvious reasons. But I also really cared about him, so I just wanted him to be healthy.

"Things were going great, and we were getting along very well. Jason and I were spending a lot of time together, and we took our first vacation after three months. I was feeling like somebody's girlfriend for the first time in years, and I was enjoying the mutual support system we'd developed. After so many near-misses, I felt like I'd finally found this fabulous guy, and the cool thing was that he'd been under my nose all along. But then I began to suspect he was cheating on me. Not with a woman, mind you, but with cigarettes. Every time we'd meet up, he'd smell like disinfectant and mint chewing gum. He never smelled like just a guy, but like someone masking something. And then I found a lighter in his pocket, which he claimed belonged to a friend. Eventually he confessed and said he was smoking socially, but that he had no intention of doing it in front of me or in our apartments.

"It wasn't just his health I was concerned about. As a former smoker, I couldn't handle the temptation. And I guess on a deeper level, his regression to smoking seemed like a betrayal of some sort, like once we'd become an item he could relax and fall back on all his old habits. It was a form of disrespect.

"Of course, addictions are hard to beat, and soon he was running down to the street to smoke whenever we hung out. While he was careful never to leave his cigarettes lying around, he couldn't always cover up the trail. The telltale sign is the kiss. It was like making out with Philip Morris. I finally had to tell him that it was either the cigarettes or me. It was his choice."

JASON'S TESTIMONY

"I was smitten with Connie from the day I first met her, in front of our office building at Third Avenue and 48th Street. Midtown never looked so good as when she was standing there. But since we worked together and I had a mid-level management position, I couldn't risk pursuing her. But the thought was there with me from day one, actually moment one. The truth is I'd always had this hunch we'd wind up together.

"While I would never wish a job loss on anyone, I was somewhat relieved when she was let go in a wave of dot-com layoffs. She was given a generous package and the layoff gave her a chance to reassess and do something she liked better. She started taking yoga, and she learned how to knit. Most important, she used the change as an impetus to quit smoking. She even inspired me to lay down my beloved Camel Lights.

"They say the right woman can make you a better man, and that seems to be true in the case of Connie. I had tried for years to give up smoking. Nothing worked: not the patch, not hypnosis. Nothing, that is, until Connie came along. I wanted us to have a chance, and I knew that meant I needed to be smoke-free. She didn't demand it or anything, but I knew she'd be happier if I wasn't smoking. So I stopped, and it wasn't that hard with her by my side. I felt so thrilled to be with her that I didn't miss the nicotine.

"But then, work got busy and my stress level went through the roof. At first I tried the chewing gum and it helped a little. I even signed up for a boxing class, thinking I could take out my aggressions elsewhere. But eventually I went back to cigarettes. I knew that Connie would be disappointed, and I tried to keep it from her, but that didn't last too long. There is only so low a man can sink before he is forced to confess the ugly truth.

"I figured she'd be mad, but that she'd understand. After all, if you love someone, you have to accept them for who they are, warts and all. Our first few months had been like a fairytale, and I know my smoking blew a dark haze over all that. But this was my reality, and she'd have to accept it. I wanted to quit again, but I felt I couldn't do it unless I was ready. And until then, honesty and good intentions would have to suffice. In a way, this desire to be open showed how close I felt. I admitted to her that I wasn't perfect, but that I was trying my best. She felt like I had gotten lazy, and that my smoking was a rebuke. But in my mind, my promise to quit once things settled down at work showed that I really envisioned her as part of my smoke-free future. I thought a little time was no biggie over the course of a possible lifetime together. And then just like that, she snuffed me out."

DSI ASSESSMENT

This case presents a unique scenario because, for Connie, cigarette smoking is something she feels she cannot compromise on, despite her feelings for Jason. For his part, Jason is in the unfortunate position of being victimized by a habit that he cannot, on some level, control. Such situations, where an external factor (such as an unexpected relocation, a death in the family, or a serious health issue) jeopardizes an otherwise happy relationship, can be devastating to the person on the other end of the new condition. In some cases, it can happen quite late in the game, like when a couple suddenly realizes they cannot synthesize disparate religious views in terms of raising children together. But in most cases the result is similar: some kind of hurdle prevents the relationship from moving forward. It is then up to the two people to determine whether they can find a way to compromise or if the deal is off.

RELATIONSHIP REHAB

→ Jason must go on a program to wean down his smoking and *quit*!

→ Connie needs to give Jason the space to quit on his own terms, and she must trust him to make good on his commitment, so he can trust her to make good on their relationship.

DATING DIAGNOSTIC

Perhaps Jason could make more of a concerted effort to quit smoking now, but corny as it sounds, he might not be "in the right place" to make such a dramatic change. Tapering down might be an interim solution, but Connie would have to be willing to put up with him through this process. As we saw from her testimony, she appears to be personalizing Jason's relapse as indicative of a decline in his feelings for her. While she may have been partially right, it's more accurate to say that Jason had de-

veloped some degree of faith and trust in the sanctity of their relationship, which is probably in need of repair. At this point, they both have
some work to do: Jason must try his best to figure out a clear-cut solution
for quitting that works for both him and Connie and then (and this is the
hard part) *stick with it!* Connie must focus on rebuilding the idealized
trust Jason had in a future with Connie.

FOLLOW-UP

A six-month follow-up found Jason and Connie happily living together
and totally smoke free. Jason said it was really hard, but as much as he
loves nicotine, he loves Connie more.

PROFILES IN COURAGE
The ARSES You Sent Packing

Because DSI cannot be everywhere at once, we'd like to tip our hats to the empowered female citizens across the nation who have the wisdom, the gumption, the nerve, and, okay, we'll say it, the balls to dump the dudes who deserve to be dumped and to engage in a special form of citizen's arrest. And so, without further ado, it is our great honor to raise our glasses: a toast to the ladies whose hunches paid off. Apprehending wrongdoers is everybody's right, obligation, and duty.

CITIZEN'S ARREST: THE CASE OF THE GUY WHO WOULD NOT GROW UP

Despite the fact that her actions were bound to make her single again at the tender age of thirty-two, Caryn Klein placed her boyfriend, thirty-five-year-old Glen Carter, under a citizen's arrest for "conducting himself in a manner unbecoming of a mature adult." The two had been dating for ten months, and the relationship was moving in a direction that suggested it might become serious. Yet Mr. Carter refused to act like a mature adult. While some of his childish antics were almost cute to Ms. Klein in the beginning, she soon grew tired of his addiction to video games, "pull my finger" fart jokes, and fantasy football leagues, especially when he began missing dates in order to engage in said activities with other male friends (all of whom, it should be noted, were single).

This, however, was only the beginning of Mr. Carter's misadventures in distended adolescence. Other indicators included his habit of dressing like a teenager (including ripped jeans and sneakers worn with laces untied), referring to Ms. Klein as his "beeyatch" and finding an excuse (for instance, one-dollar beers) to go drinking most nights of the week. Ms. Klein grew tired of his habits, but continued to put up with him because she felt she might be able to rehabilitate him, to tap his "inner adult." There were moments when she saw glimmers of the future Mr. Carter. His job as a commodities trader seemed to demand that he act in a semi-adult manner—though it should be noted that Mr. Carter and his cohorts stuffed more than their fair share of bills down sequin thongs.

This immaturity was most evident in Mr. Carter's inability to demonstrate even the piddling murmur of an emotional pulse. While Mr. Carter was able to feign interest in some of the things that mattered to Ms. Klein, such as acoustic women's folk-rock and animal rescue activism, he was unable to express his deeper feelings. When pressed, he'd turn on the television, talk about dinner or, when all else failed, shove straws up his nostrils and sing, "I am the walrus," until Ms. Klein either laughed or stomped out of the apartment in desperate frustration. Despite this limitation, Mr. Carter made boisterous claims about his desire for a future with Ms. Klein.

This slow-declining limbo went on for several months until Ms. Klein finally began to realize Mr. Carter would never change. Ms. Klein phoned DSI to let us know her plans and then apprehended Mr. Carter. The arrest was made during a rousing game of Grand Theft Auto, so he was not difficult to capture. In fact, the arrest records note that he was docile and placid, and that his eyes were glazed over. DSI eventually took custody of Mr. Carter, who is currently serving a sentence of three to five years for his crimes. Ms. Klein was deputized shortly thereafter and has participated in the apprehension of more than a dozen ARSEs thus far.

THREE:

THE WELL-GROOMED MAN

THE CASE OF THE GUY WHO MIGHT BE GAY

THE DSI 911

At 9 A.M. on September 14, 2004, the FBI (Federal Bureau of Intimacy) routed a panicked call to Team DSI. It was from the Dating DUPE (Desperately Under Pressure to Evaluate), one Ms. Stephanie Parker of Los Angeles, California, following a three-day holiday weekend spent with the ARSE (Anti-Relationship Suspect Examinee), her purported "boyfriend" of two months, Michael Rogers.

Ms. Parker reported that Mr. Rogers failed to make any sexual advances toward her physical person over the weekend in question, which involved a variety of semi-romantic activities, including a sunset stroll along the beach, the viewing of a film that involved tastefully sequenced adult situations, and faux complaints of muscle aches designed to encourage a massage. Despite these efforts, Ms. Parker failed to inspire Mr. Rogers to "make a final move." Having reached a point of quiet desperation, Ms. Parker turned the case over to DSI to determine whether Mr. Rogers is, in fact, gay.

PRELIMINARY DIAGNOSIS

Based on the DSI team's initial observations, we determined that this was a case of Metrosexualis Over-Dosius (MOD), a common condition that is often confused with homosexuality, particularly prevalent in urban areas of the United States.

MOD is a dating-related disorder whereby a man presumed to be heterosexual displays certain behaviors that, combined with sexual passivity, lead women to accuse him of being gay.

DSI's National Evidence Relationship Database (NERD) tracking system has revealed a marked increase in the number of such cases in the past five years. This situation is partially attributable to television shows like *Queer Eye for the Straight Guy* and to a measurable, overall improvement in male fashion, grooming, personal style, emotional well-being, health, and interior design panache. Despite the evident benefits to MOD-suspected men and the women who love them, this mammoth swell in male sensitivity has added a new layer of confusion to dating and heterosexual relationships.

PARALLEL CASE ANECDOTALS

A sampling of testimony from other recent DSI investigations into MOD illustrate the modern state of gender dynamics.

> "I keep dating all these guys who have more 'design' products in their bathrooms than I do. Sure, I want a sensitive boyfriend, but David takes longer to get ready than my little sister on prom night. I swear sometimes I think he's gay."
>
> **—Margaret, 26**

> "The dating landscape is tricky to navigate these days, because women claim they want men who have feminine qualities. But Sarah yells at me for not being enough of a caveman in bed. It's like she wants a wolf in Paul Smith clothing."
>
> **—Mark, 35**

"I'm not really sure what to do these days. I'm your average khakis and light beer kind of guy, but it seems a dying breed. Everywhere I turn, queer eyes are trying to change me. But when I listen to them, the women I meet tell me they wish I were more like a guy's guy."

—Steve, 33

CASE SPECIFICS

THE DUPE: Stephanie Parker
Age: 32
Location: Los Angeles, CA
Occupation: Screenwriter
Hair: Brown
Eyes: Hazel
Height: 5'4"
Weight: 130

RELATIONSHIP RAP SHEET/EX FILES

Past Serious Relationships: 5
Total Number of Sexual Partners: 9
Exes Still in Contact: 3

Interpersonal Infractions

Ms. Parker has a long history of not returning phone calls or emails from men who show what she calls "excessive" or "clingy" interest. Conversely, Ms. Parker has a propensity to exhibit similar behavior patterns when she engages in sexual activity early on in a relationship followed by a lack of communication by the gentleman thereafter. When she is interested in a potential mate who shows the least bit of disinterest in her, she becomes sexually aggressive and emotionally demanding (including several DWI [Dialing While Intoxicated] incidents). If another date is requested too quickly after said first sexual encounter, however, Ms. Parker loses interest.

Mating Misdemeanors

April 2, 1993

Faked an orgasm with her college boyfriend, a star pitcher on the school's baseball team. She did not want him to think her less sexy than his last girlfriend, who purported to have multiple orgasms just from watching him swing his proverbial bat. This was the first of many such instances where she faked orgasm and sacrificed her own sexual gratification.

September–December 1995

Led on a college study partner, Marvin Ratner (now a dot-com tycoon), by making out with him on numerous Saturday nights so he would continue to tutor her in computer science, in which she was skimming a "C" average.

Flirtatious Felonies

May 15, 2001

Insulted the sexual prowess of a man she had been dating for three weeks during a surprise birthday party thrown by his best friends, referring to him as "the little engine that couldn't," and "small fry."

August 3, 2004

Broke up with a boyfriend because her friends called him "geeky," despite the fact that she really enjoyed his company, and he treated her better than any of her exes.

Psychographic Thumbnail

Raised in a "traditional" household, Ms. Parker is the middle child of three girls, all trained in the cosmetic and domestic arts by their mother—a purported "domestic engineer"—and discouraged from pursuing careers inconsistent with their duties as future homemakers. Ms. Parker has no conscious recollection of seeing her mother without two coats of "Passion Pink" L'Oreal lipstick and waterproof mascara (used to mask any and all feminine outbursts). Ms. Parker's mother made a habit of receiving her husband at the door each night in a pink peignoir and matching marabou slippers, with a martini and newspaper in hand and a reheated casserole on the stove, no matter how late he arrived from the local bank he managed, no questions asked. Ms. Parker's older sister got married during her senior year of art school and has two children and no independent source of income, while her younger sister, a piano teacher, lives in Northampton, Massachusetts, with her "special friend" Libby, and twelve other "wymyn artists."

Ms. Parker's history reveals a pattern of dating overtly masculine men who show below-average levels of sensitivity, communication, and feminine qualities. She also suffers from a chronic tendency to fake orgasm during sexual intercourse, placing a premium on her desirability and "hot-factor," often to the detriment of her own gratification. She generally rates the success of a romantic encounter by how much a partner appears to desire her, with little to no regard for how much she wants them in return. She is flattered when a man is so eager for her that he dispenses with preliminaries. This often leads to frustration and angry outbursts in lieu of genuine communication regarding her unfulfilled sexual needs.

In most of her past relationships, Ms. Parker cited a lack of communication as the prime reason for the breakup. Two years of cognitive therapy have led her to the conclusion that she has been seeking to replicate the kind of relationship her parents had. Her terror at such revelation (shrieked Ms. Parker: "Ew, the horror, the horror") led her to seek out more progressive partners with feminine qualities or, as she puts it, "sensitive types" like Mr. Rogers.

THE ARSE: Michael Rogers
Age: 35
Location: West Hollywood, CA
Occupation: public relations executive/spin instructor
Hair: Brown

Eyes: Blue
Height: 5'10"
Weight: 168

RELATIONSHIP RAP SHEET/EX FILES

Past Serious Relationships: 2
Total Number of Sexual Partners: 27
Exes Still in Contact: 11

Interpersonal Infractions

1988–2005

Neglected to call numerous women after the third date despite the discussion of future weekend getaways.

Mating Misdemeanors

March 14, 1997

Was accused by a girlfriend of getting too hot and bothered during football games and for a particular penchant for watching the tight ends on the TV while engaged in a posterior poke of her person. During one such heated encounter, he accidentally called her by an ex-girlfriend's name. [*Note:* The "ex-girlfriend" was named "Chris."]

May 11, 1999

Broke up with a woman he'd been dating for three months because their "seasons" didn't match. (He was a winter, while she was a spring, which went against the winter-summer/spring-fall ideal fashion combination.)

January 1, 2003

Abandoned an attractive blind date at a New Year's Eve party to continue the evening with a group of male friends. [*Note:* The evening included a visit to VickTorio's Secret, a local transvestite bar, which Mr. Rogers claimed was for "campy" purposes only.]

Flirtatious Felonies

May 5, 1993

Although supposedly engaged in a monogamous relationship, committed three counts of infidelity during the first summer of college while working as a counselor at Camp Mohegan. His coconspirator, another counselor, was unaware Mr. Rogers was "taken." Upon paying him a surprise visit, his college sweetheart screamed, "For God's sake, she's built like a twelve-year-old boy!"

January 1, 1996

Briefly dated a clinically obese, slightly cross-eyed heiress from Atlanta with whom he spent a good deal of time shopping at Barney's on her platinum card and getting side-by-side cellulite treatments at various high-end day spas.

August 5, 2001

Broke off a two-year relationship via Blackberry, citing "differences in long-term goals" and his desire to get in touch with himself more before making such a serious commitment.

Psychographic Thumbnail

An only child, Mr. Rogers was raised by a single mother, whose only boyfriend disappeared when she refused to abort an unplanned pregnancy. A bookkeeper at her church, Ms. Rogers never dated, telling her son he was "the only man in her life," other than Jesus. Referring to both men as her "best friends," she consistently sought his advice regarding clothing and furniture purchases, and called him her "sous chef" in the kitchen. Rather than playing sports with other boys, Mr. Rogers spent Saturdays (his mother's only day off) listening to Broadway musicals and taking long walks in the local botanical gardens.

Although he went to college close to his Michigan home, Mr. Rogers ultimately moved to Hollywood to pursue a film-related career, causing both him and his mother considerable duress. He continues to speak with his mother on the phone daily and endeavors to visit her at least once a month for shopping, theater, and gourmet dining. Ever the dutiful son, he sends his mother a weekly bouquet of fresh flowers and secretly pads her bank account.

Mr. Rogers shows no outward symptoms of homophobia. Moreover, he exhibits the telltale signs of "shellshock" from earlier dating mishaps and a previous inclination to three-night stands with members of the opposite sex. He is comfortable in describing other men as attractive and spends time with openly gay male friends. His priors show a discomfort with extending intimate relations beyond sexual interaction (i.e., the third date drop-off effect) or postponing sex with women he truly likes.

Mr. Rogers' profile is consistent with many men his age, particularly those who have been raised in female-dominant homes. His tendency to stop dating on or around the third date suggests intimacy insecurities and/or a sense of guilt/reluctance about potentially "displacing" his mother as "the only woman in his life."

RELATIONSHIP RECONNAISSANCE

The DSI investigation revealed that Mr. Rogers and Ms. Parker were introduced to each other by a mutual friend, one Monica Rosenstein. Ms. Rosenstein, an interior designer, has known Ms. Parker since college, and the two see each other socially every few months. Ms. Rosenstein and Mr. Rogers are relatively new acquaintances, having met at a spin class that Mr. Rogers teaches in his spare time.

Ms. Rosenstein has a history of attempting to set up Ms. Parker with eligible men, with what should be noted as "largely calamitous results." Aware that Ms. Parker often complains that the men she meets lack a certain amount of sensitivity, Ms. Rosenstein has attempted to cull from her pool of bachelor friends who work in fields that are not typically "masculine." Ms. Rosenstein and Mr. Rogers are mere acquaintances, and it was clear to team DSI that her matchmaking was undertaken without any knowledge of Mr. Rogers' dating history or personal preferences.

According to Ms. Rosenstein, she found Mr. Rogers "adorable" and "perfect for Stephanie, who needs to stop dating those meatheads she's been seeing for so long." When asked if she thought the fact that he taught a spinning class was odd, she answered that it "gave him a unique insight into women's fitness issues." She also added he was well-known in the women's locker room as the dude with the "tight glutes."

Steve Thompson, a friend of Mr. Rogers who met Ms. Parker, indicated that he was "surprised" that Michael would go for her type, noting that "she seemed a bit aggressive for Michael, who likes to take things at his own pace."

DATE SCENE RECONSTRUCTION

The DSI team identified three key dates meriting examination:

Date Two: Dinner and a Movie

LOCALE: Chez Brigitte Restaurant

Synopsis: Mr. Rogers carefully avoided ogling Ms. Parker's well-supported décolletage. After Ms. Parker "accidentally" spilled whipped cream on her cleavage and proceeded to dab and lick it off her fingers, Mr. Rogers immediately cleared his throat and resituated his napkin on his crotch. Nonetheless his consistent eye contact and body language (leaning in toward her and listening attentively throughout the meal) indicated active interest.

Witness Testimony: According to a member of the wait staff, Mr. Rogers made eye contact with an attractive woman at the next table when Ms. Parker went to "powder her nose." The bathroom attendant remembered him as the one with the "male manicure who left me a twenty-smacker tip."

Date Five: Kiss Me You Fool

LOCALE: Outdoor Concert/The Santa Monica Pier

Synopsis: During a romantic twilight stroll by the pier after an outdoor concert. Ms. Parker wrapped her arm around Mr. Rogers' waist, eliciting the following remark: "Do you think I've put on a few pounds? I'm feeling a little pudgy around the middle lately." Ms. Parker assured him he was looking svelte, but felt rebuffed and turned off. Hoping to elicit a more "masculine" reaction, she backed him against the amphitheater wall and attempted to kiss him. Mr. Rogers pecked her on the forehead, however, and awkwardly disentangled himself from her embrace.

Witness Testimony: Tourists wandering in the same area indicated that it was crowded and that Mr. Rogers looked taken aback by the public nature of Ms. Parker's affection.

Date Nine: A Very Long Weekend

LOCALE: Residence of Ms. Stephanie Parker

Synopsis: After a pleasant dinner at a local Mexican restaurant, where Ms. Parker drank several margaritas and Mr. Rogers, the "designated driver," drank nothing, the couple retired to Ms. Parker's apartment. Ms. Parker played a Metallica CD (which Mr. Rogers detested) and proceeded to put the moves on Mr. Rogers on her leather sofa (which Mr. Rogers criticized as sanctifying cruelty to cows). Mr. Rogers excused himself to use the bathroom. When he returned a few minutes later, he sat down on the recliner across from Ms. Parker. Determined not to be put off, Ms. Parker promptly deposited herself in her date's lap. (Trouser Tenting Assessment [TTA] results indicated that Mr. Rogers did not achieve an expected level of erectile arousal during a variety of couch-based cuddling sessions.) Mr. Rogers jumped out of the chair on contact and claimed he had bad indigestion from his undercooked whole wheat veggie burrito, leaving the apartment shortly thereafter.

Witness Testimony: Ms. Parker's doorman indicated that she'd clearly been drinking and was hanging "all over the poor sap." An elevator operator who saw the two suggested that Mr. Rogers appeared "standoffish" and slightly unsettled by Ms. Parker's slovenly attention.

FORENSIC ASSESSMENT AND EVIDENTIARY ANALYSIS

Physical Evidence

A careful investigation of Mr. Rogers' home revealed the following.

Clothing

→ Selection indicates a tendency toward understated designer labels and an aversion to middle-market selections, such as The Gap.

→ Shoe-wear analysis reveals that athletic shoes in collection are worn solely for social purposes and include Marc Jacobs sneakers and Miu-Miu faux bowling shoes.

→ Neutral color palette suggests a heightened sensitivity to garish styles.

→ Denim selections exclude Levis and tend toward $200 haute couture brands such as Paper, Denim & Cloth.

→ Pants, button-downs, and polos were folded along natural seams and organized by season, textile, and color.

→ DSI sweeps were unable to find any garments containing polyester fibers, or traces thereof.

Furnishings

→ Substantial collection of mid-century modern furnishings include an Eames lounge chair and several Herman Miller pieces along with rugged, mission-style antiques that are simultaneously "masculine" yet design-conscious.

➤ Bed linens were 600-thread count Egyptian cotton with shams and decorative pillows neatly arranged, though color scheme was decidedly "masculine" in a navy damask weave.

➤ There is a noticeable lack of black leather and/or fluorescent lighting.

➤ Artwork and photography is carefully hung, with an attention to frame choice. Red flag on the autographed Bernadette Peters *Gypsy* poster.

Personal Effects

➤ Books on shelves cover a wide range of current genres and appear to have actually been read. Baseline comparative profiling indicates a lower than average count in the action thriller area but a higher than average count in the self-help genre (with a focus on sex and relationship titles), and a red-flag on a dog-eared copy of Simone de Beauvoir's *The Second Sex*.

➤ Musical choices were broad, though heavy in Broadway scores, with a red flag beside a shelf devoted to "Favorite Divas," that included Edith Piaf, Joni Mitchell, Beverly Hills singing swing, and Barbra Streisand in *Yentl*.

➤ Kitchen and pantry were well-stocked, with an alphabetized spice rack that offered four varieties of thyme.

➤ Two shelves of Italian cookbooks were located beside a well-worn copy of *Moosewood Cookbook Classics*.

➤ Checkbook was balanced and bills appeared to be organized by due date.

➤ Grooming items in bathroom suggested a recent splurge at Bliss with two different moisturizers and a toner.

➤ Condom count revealed the acquisition of prophylactics within the last three months (based on date of expiration), but included a few varieties in rainbow colors (consistent with bachelor party favors).

Forensic Metrics

Latent Intimacy for Males Potential (LIMP) Test

Because the evidence and testimony as presented did not allow team DSI to make a conclusive determination on Mr. Rogers' sexuality, we had to undertake a LIMP test. The test assigns a rating to an ARSE's level of sensitivity and feminized qualities, utilizing both external physical indicators (clothing choices, tone of voice, musical tastes) and internal emotional readings. The test provides a range of male intimacy potential, from Stuffed Shirt Straight Arrow to Village People Wannabe.

Mr. Roger's LIMP test results indicated that his feminine sensibilities were well within "normal" range and not proof of a particular sexual orientation.

DSI FINDING

Investigation of the couple's dating DNA (their individual and collective dating "fingerprints") indicates that Mr. Rogers has a history of moving gradually with regard to intimate relationships. Mr. Rogers' past indicates a readiness to jump in the sack with someone he doesn't care about, but a reluctance to "make a move" when a desire (and threat) of true emotion presents itself (owing to fears of intimacy and a desire not to replicate his father's disappearing act with someone he cares about).

Mr. Rogers' failure to do his third date disappearing act demonstrates that he regards Ms. Parker as a possible candidate for a long-term relationship. By labeling Mr. Rogers' sexual orientation suspect, Ms. Parker turned a blind eye to his and her own intimacy and compatibility issues. Her compensatory tendency to turn up the heat and take the reigns sexually only exacerbated Mr. Rogers' fears. Based on her dating history and family of origin patterns, Ms. Parker's file has been modified to include a "Talk the Talk, Won't Walk the Walk" designation with regard to her stated desires to date "more sensitive men."

The physical evidence and forensic analysis in this case indicate that, while Mr. Rogers does indeed have certain qualities that could be described as feminine, he is by no means gay. Our conclusion is that Mr. Rogers is, indeed, a heterosexual man with good fashion sense, a broad interest in the arts, excellent hygiene, and profound intimacy issues.

RELATIONSHIP REHAB

We have determined that Mr. Rogers and Ms. Parker have enough chemistry and commonality of interests (including shopping and cooking, though not music) to continue forward in a relationship. To this end, we have given both parties the following tip sheet:

→ Ms. Parker should reassess her stereotypical gender views and realize that just because a man is fashionable and feminine does not mean he's gay.

→ Ms. Parker should try to back down and be more comfortable with intimate situations that do not culminate in sex without questioning her own attractiveness or maligning Mr. Rogers' masculinity.

→ Ms. Parker should be more aware of how her own insecurities play into her need for male approval and learn how to communicate her needs more openly and effectively.

→ Ms. Parker should challenge her ostensible desire not to replicate her parents' marriage, given her repeated selections of typically masculine, insensitive men. If she does want to engage in a more egalitarian relationship, she should embrace the opportunity for true intimacy and confront her own gender assumptions.

→ Mr. Rogers should spend some time in therapy to deal with his feelings of guilt toward his mother and how his fear of replicating his father's behavior is impeding his ability to mix sex and intimacy.

→ Mr. Rogers should be more comfortable being sexual with Ms. Parker and be more cognizant of her needs for physical affection and assurance, even if he prefers to take it slow.

→ Mr. Rogers should funnel his evolved aesthetic sensibility into picking out sexy lingerie for Ms. Parker and creating the perfect setting for romantic encounters.

→ Mr. Rogers must learn to wear the pants in the relationship with a bit more authority, even if this means trying on a pair of Dockers every now and again.

DATING DIAGNOSTIC

Men are asked to be sensitive and feminized, but at the same time, they are often expected to be the hunter-gatherers and alpha members of a relationship. Women are increasingly pressured to look or act as "wild" as the women on their partners' proverbial hard drives and tend to equate lack of sexual arousal as an indication that they are falling short of some celluloid silicon ideal.

In many such cases, women overcompensate for a male's perceived lack of interest by becoming more aggressive, turning every intimate situation into an opportunity for the male to make a move. Such actions, however, often turn men off or increase performance anxiety, leading to a spiral of miscommunication.

By focusing primarily on when and how often a man makes a move, or by jumping to the conclusion that such a man is gay or fatally metrosexual, women are neglecting to focus on larger issues, such as intimacy, as well as depriving themselves of many of the very qualities they've ostensibly desired, such as heightened sensitivity and common interests in health, aesthetics, culture, and the like.

While we tend to say we want "equal" relationships, we are not necessarily turned on by some aspects of our new roles, which fail to play into historic tropes of desire. Men who try to be more communicative and sensitive often find themselves overtly or covertly derided as effeminate. Women who are encouraged to be more sexually aggressive may be disheartened to discover that this license extends no further than traditional male fantasy allows. Gauging the "signs" of sexual attraction and interpreting the rules of dating have never been more confusing. But, in this moment of dynamic transformation, we have the opportunity to move beyond rigid polemics and pick and choose whom we want to be, and be with. This requires giving ourselves, and our partners, the freedom to express our likes, dislikes, passions, foibles, sensitivities, fantasies, and phobias without censure. Only then can we figure out if we truly mesh and work toward creating greater intimacy and compatibility based on who we are, not who we are supposed to be.

FOLLOW-UP

At the one-year check-in the DSI team learned that Mr. Rogers had ended his relationship with Ms. Parker, claiming they were not right for one another. He had since gotten engaged to a woman he'd had met three months prior at an orchid festival, though Ms. Parker contends that the woman is a beard and he is gay. Ms. Parker, though still single, recently enjoyed a promising third date with a male nurse that included a genuine orgasm and a follow-up call.

IS YOUR GUY A MOD (METROSEXUALIS OVER-DOSIOUS) OR HID (HOMOSEXUALIS IN DENIUS)?*

BEHAVIORAL TENDENCIES	MOD	HID
Has a well-stocked closet featuring designer labels on wood frame hangers	X	X
Relies heavily on expensive grooming aids	X	X
Displays thermodynamic climate control sensitivity	X	X
Constantly frets over his brand of hair gel	X	X
BEHAVIORAL TENDENCIES	**MOD**	**HID**
Is able to discern female shoe brands at a distance of 10 yards	X	X
TiVos *Oprah* and/or *Trading Spaces*	X	
Displays no outward desire to follow professional sports	X	X
Discusses gourmet cooking techniques and holds a fetishistic regard for Gaggenau and Garland appliances	X	X
Prefers a weeklong spa visit (with massage by exotic natives) over a trip to Vegas	X	
Has back issues of *Martha Stewart Living*		X

*Results may prove tongue-in-cheek, unless of course there is evidence of other male tongues in said cheek.

SEXUAL BEHAVIORS

Considers normal feminine sexual appetite excessive	X	
Does not grope, taunt, or ogle early on in a relationship	X	
Doesn't initiate sex	X	X
Visits gay bars routinely, claiming he's there to hang out with his gay college friend(s)		X
Possesses a large gay porn collection		X
Hypothesizes on which male celebrities are closeted	X	
Homophobic		X
Attracted to women with boyish physiques	X	X
Excessive interest in anal pleasuring	X	X
Enjoys being called "pretty" or "beautiful" by both women and men	X	X

DSI MOST WANTED FUGITIVE

WANTED FOR:

VALUING SEX ABOVE ALL OTHER ASPECTS OF A RELATIONSHIP; BASING SEXUAL IDEALS ON IMAGES DERIVED FROM PORNOGRAPHIC FILMS AND WEB SITES; CONSISTENTLY ATTEMPTING TO PERSUADE HIS GIRLFRIEND TO ENGAGE IN A THREESOME

Zachary Thompson

Aliases: Z-Boy; Zach Attack; Zac the Zipper; ThreeForTheHoney (his apparent screen name on several adult swinger sites)

DESCRIPTION

Date of Birth: 1977

Place of Birth: Pasadena, CA

Height: 5' 9" to 5' 11"

Weight: Approximately 170

Build: Muscular

Hair: Blonde

Eyes: Blue

Complexion: Light

Sex: Male

Nationality: American

Occupation: Advertising executive

Remarks: Mr. Thompson is a clever and quick-witted fugitive, and his brilliant, highly maneuvered escapes from DSI are a testament to his ability to persuade girlfriends and partners that he is more than a sexually motivated predator. He is known for a heinous tendency to quote Anaïs Nin, *Story of O*, and the Marquis de Sade in an effort to induce women to engage in activities gleaned from Internet porn sites. He tends to hang out in upscale coffee houses and book stores, singling out women who peruse the erotica section.

Scars and Marks: Has a birthmark shaped like the state of Rhode Island on his left calf, wears a goatee, and has a shaved head.

CAUTION

THOMPSON HAS BEEN CATEGORIZED A DEADLY MENACE DUE TO HIS UNCANNY ABILITY TO SIMULATE THE BEHAVIORS OF A THOUGHTFUL, INTELLIGENT HUMAN BEING CAPABLE OF GENUINE AFFECTION AND LASTING COMMITMENT.

THIS INDIVIDUAL IS CONSIDERED HIGHLY PERVERTED IN A MANNER THAT IS SUGGESTIVE OF AN INABILITY TO FORM MATURE RELATIONSIPS; HE IS ALSO ARMED WITH A HIDDEN VIDEO CAMERA IN HIS ABODE, PERCHED ABOVE HIS MIRROR CANOPIED WATERBED.

IF YOU HAVE ANY INFORMATION CONCERNING THIS PERSON, PLEASE CONTACT YOUR *LOCAL DSI OFFICE*

REWARD

Intimacy Advocates of America is offering a reward of up to $200,000 for information leading to the apprehension and conviction of Zachary Thompson. The Baudelaire Society is offering an additional $500 reward for disseminating altered literary excerpts over the Internet that blaspheme the good names of French poets.

FOUR:

THE PERMANENT MISTRESS

THE CASE OF THE FOOL WHO FELL
FOR A MARRIED MAN

THE DSI 911

Team DSI received a frenetic call from one Ms. Heather Jenkins, who professed that her strong emotional attachment to a married man with two children was spinning out of control. While she didn't doubt that his feelings for her were genuine, she was distraught over his failure to make good on his promise to leave his wife. Said Ms. Jenkins to our intake officer: "He told me his marriage was on the rocks the day we met, and that he was in the process of filing for divorce. But that was a long time ago, and I don't see any signs that what he said is true. I mean, do you really go on a two-week trip to the Bahamas with your family just for the sake of appearances? What gives already? Is he really going to leave her or am I totally deluding myself?"

PRELIMINARY DIAGNOSIS

For those women who labor under the starry-eyed delusion that Mr. I Belong to Somebody Else will gracefully ease into Mr. Mine, there is a certain condition called Mistress Madness that develops. This begins with the inherent denial that the other person is unavailable, requiring an irrational leap of faith to believe our lover can or should "belong" to us. In so doing, the preoccupation with the immediate obstacle to happiness—his marriage—overshadows other compatibility factors that would otherwise come into play.

Such is the situation at hand, which DSI has diagnosed as a classic case of Mistress Madness, with an associative "crisis in rationalization." Ms. Jenkins is clearly suffering from aggravated emotional denial compounded by thwarted desire.

PARALLEL CASE ANECDOTALS

"I still feel scorned about being the 'other woman.' It's something that I regret, but the feelings were very real. He kept telling me he was going to leave his wife. And then one day, *five years later*, I woke and realized nothing was going to change."

—Lillian, 33

"To be honest, I don't even know for sure that I even really liked him, but that didn't stop me from wanting what I couldn't have."

—Katrina, 40

"When a you date a married man, on a basic level he has to constantly convince you that his essential nature is not that of a lying, cheating snake, which predisposes you to all sorts of rationalizations and justifications of his behavior, because at heart he really is a lying snake or else he wouldn't be cheating on his wife."

—Abigail, 35

"Sex with a married man is often really hot because of all the sneaking around. There's always a sense of urgency and risk of getting caught. And there's none of the boring domestic stuff to go with it. It's like all hotels and hot weekends away without having to stress about meeting his folks or whether or not he does his own laundry."

—Cathy, 29

CASE SPECIFICS

The Dupe: Heather Jenkins
Age: 29
Location: Boston, MA
Occupation: Law firm associate
Hair: Auburn
Eyes: Green
Height: 5'6"
Weight: 142

RELATIONSHIP RAP SHEET/EX FILES

Past Serious Relationships: 4
Total Number of Sexual Partners: 9
Exes Still in Contact: 5

Interpersonal Infractions

→ Has a history of dating men who are not right for her, beginning with a twenty-four-year-old car mechanic when she was in junior high school

→ Craves romantic and sexual excitement and grows bored easily in relationships

→ After college, she developed a preference for older men in high-powered positions

Mating Misdemeanors

August 2002

Meets a divorced senior partner, with a reputation for being "a woman-izer," during a two-week due diligence assignment at a satellite office in Chicago. After a few brief smiles, she proceeds to corner him in his office one afternoon, risking her job in the process. They begin to see each other on occasional weekends, without discussing whether they are free to see other people (she is monogamous). He tells her he would never get married again, but she refuses to believe him and calls him "silly." She surprises him with an impromptu visit one weeknight and discovers him in bed with his twenty-two-year-old paralegal.

July 2003

After getting too much criticism from her friends about her taste in men, she decides to go out with a friend of a friend from college, a smart, at-tractive architect in a successful Cambridge practice. They appear to have a lot in common, a love of Led Zeppelin and Jimi Hendrix, a taste for ethnic cuisine, a yen for adventure that leads them to go parasailing, sky-diving, deep-sea diving, and bungee jumping. But Ms. Jenkins contends the sex isn't hot enough, despite the fact that they have sex everywhere (including the backseat of a taxi, on the top of a mountain, and at high tide on the Nantucket shore). She accuses him of cheating on her, and when he swears his undying love for her, Ms. Jenkins breaks up with him for being "too clingy."

April 2004

Her shy, Catholic-raised boyfriend confides some of his secret sexual fan-tasies, after months of needling encouragement. After he admits that he kind of "digs the idea of watching *her* with another woman," Ms. Jenkins hires a prostitute to come to her apartment as a surprise thirtieth birthday present. Although her boyfriend hardly looks at the other woman, who is fairly attractive in a drugstore-blonde sort of way, she tells him that she wants to watch him touch the woman "down there." When he finally agrees, she gets furious and stomps out the door in tears, crying, "You filthy pervert: I can't believe you call yourself a Christian and then betrayed me with a cheap whore. What would your mother think if I told her?"

Flirtatious Felonies

November 1999

Tells her law-school boyfriend of five months she doesn't believe in monogamy and encourages him to "enjoy his sexual freedom, too." When he expresses no particular inclination to see other people, she tells him that her best friend has a huge crush on him. Although flattered, he informs her he's happy with her and "not interested." She subsequently announces she is going to a bar with some girlfriends to pick up guys, and tells her best friend to go over and seduce him wearing something "really slinky." In a fit of revenge, her boyfriend makes out with her best friend, but then sends her away. Ms. Jenkins breaks up with him the next morning, screaming, "I always knew you were a cheating bastard!"

August 2002

Initiates an affair with the married managing partner of her law firm, and then calls it off after meeting his family at the holiday office party. Plagued with sudden pangs of guilt over being a home-wrecker, she promises herself it won't ever happen again.

January 2003

Gets involved with a bartender at a hip downtown club (after a rousing one-night stand), who is well known for making the rounds. Convinced he's "cheating on her," she hacks into his email and finds racy correspondence referring to recent "hot dates" with other women. When she confronts him, he says, "I didn't think we were exclusive," at which point she gives him an ultimatum: "If I catch you again, we're through." A week later, she intercepts another naughty letter describing a lurid V.I.P. room encounter from a woman with the handle, LollyPop@hotmail.com. Incensed, she demands an explanation. He replies, "I never said we were exclusive." She concludes, "Well, it better not happen again or we're through." This continues for another four months until at last he decides he "really wants to make a go of it," at which point she responds: "It's already too late. You've destroyed my trust."

Psychographic Thumbnail

Ms. Jenkins has a history of pursuing unavailable men. She grows bored easily and her desire for excitement leads her to create trouble where none exists. She has clear-cut symptoms of commitment-phobia and appears to enjoy the element of the "chase" more than the calm of long-term companionship.

Raised primarily by her mother after her father, a senior partner at a law firm, left the family for a young receptionist, Ms. Jenkins assumes that all men are prone to cheat and abandon their families given the proper incentive, and that it's just a matter of time before they show their real stripes. This negative opinion of men causes her to keep a distance in relationships and never to let her guard down. She has also displayed a history of being passive in relationships, and of thinking she can "convert" men into something more than they are. This often leads her to choose men who are "wrong" for her. But the addiction to the excitement outweighs her good sense. She prefers high-powered, older men, though she assumes that they are the least trustworthy and most inclined to cheat.

The Arse: Martin Robertson
Age: 44
Location: Brookline, MA
Occupation: Senior partner, law firm
Hair: Brownish gray
Eyes: Blue

Height: 6'
Weight: 190

RELATIONSHIP RAP SHEET/EX FILES

Past Serious Relationships: 2
Total Number of Sexual Partners: 3
Exes Still in Contact: 1

Interpersonal Infractions

→ Has a history of being incommunicative and avoiding romantic confrontations

→ Tends to let women lead in relationships, although he gives the illusion of being in control

→ Intuitive talent for telling women precisely what they want to hear, whether he means it or not

Mating Misdemeanors

November 1985
Announced to his high school sweetheart in front of her entire extended family at Thanksgiving dinner that he intends to "stay true forever," despite the fact that he knew she was not "the one."

January 1993
Fired a Danish au pair after his wife caught him sneaking a peak at her while she was taking a shower. Mr. Robertson apologized profusely and later spoke with his father about the incident, deeply ashamed at his lewd behavior. His father advised him to renew his vows to his wife before the eyes of God, which he did, at a small family service at the church where they were married. All was forgiven, and the subject was never brought up again.

Flirtatious Felonies

March 1998

While on a business trip to Chicago, Mr. Robertson was propositioned by a saucy young waitress at the hotel restaurant. Having had a few too many martinis, he accepted her offer of a back massage in his hotel room. He then engaged in an unprecedented two-night stand, promising her he'd be back once a month on business, and leaving her with an expensive necklace as proof. He avoided the hotel on all future business trips and never told his father or wife about it. He did speak with the pastor at his church about his moral lapse, however, and he was advised to forgive himself and try to be a better husband and father in the future.

Psychographic Thumbnail

Mr. Robertson was raised in a sexually conservative home. Mr. Robertson's mother was a schoolteacher who worked throughout his childhood. His father, an attorney in private practice, was home for dinner each night by 7:00 P.M. "come hell or high water." Both Mr. Robertson and his sister were encouraged to pursue careers and to consider family their top priority. Premarital sex was frowned upon, as was casual dating. Mr. Robertson's older sister joined her father's law practice, after marrying her first and only boyfriend and having two children. Mr. Robertson had limited sexual experience before marrying his college sweetheart, who remained a virgin until they were engaged.

He and his wife, a part-time social worker at a local youth center, have been together for nearly two decades. While he claims he still loves her, he has recently joked with male friends that she is "as hot as a cold dishrag" in bed and that "her idea of kinky is doing it before the *Tonight Show*." Not counting Ms. Jenkins, Mr. Robertson had one other extramarital affair with a waitress he met on a business trip. While he has had ample opportunity to "play around," Mr. Robertson expresses open contempt for the kind of men who go to "cheesy strip clubs," and is proud of his reputation as a "real family man." Mr. Robertson's history indicates that he avoids sexual temptation as well as emotional confrontation, and avoids upsetting the status quo.

Up until Ms. Jenkins came along, Mr. Robertson worked a lot of hours, but when he wasn't at work, he was home with his wife and two sons. Ms. Jenkins came onto him at a conference in Miami after a cocktail party. Finding himself in a hotel room with an attractive young woman from another law firm, he gave in. The depth of his feelings surprised them both.

RELATIONSHIP RECONNAISSANCE

Ms. Jenkins and Mr. Robertson first met four years ago, when Ms. Jenkins was a summer associate at the law firm where Mr. Jenkins is a senior partner. During the tenure of her summer rotations through the various departments, she spent a great deal of time with Mr. Robertson, who was the hiring partner for the firm and hence was expected to attend the majority of lunches and dinners with the summer associates. After she graduated from law school, she was offered a position by Mr. Robertson at the firm, but turned it down in favor of a firm that focused more heavily on intellectual property, her chosen field of concentration. Mr. Robertson tendered a glowing recommendation and the two remained in occasional email contact thereafter.

Two years ago, they unexpectedly found themselves at a patent and trademark conference in Miami. Having fallen somewhat out of touch, they spent several hours chatting over cocktails, enjoying a lively discussion about literature, restaurants, movies, and favorite authors, taking amusement in how much their taste diverged. Ms. Jenkins was openly flirtatious, which Mr. Robertson found refreshing and attractive. She walked him to his room after the party and asked if she could join him for a nightcap in his suite. When he nervously invited her in, Ms. Jenkins stripped down to her bra and panties and gave him his "very first lap dance."

Since that night, they've been seeing each other at least twice a week for extended "lunch dates," which usually take place at a motel. Mr.

Robertson told his wife he was assigned to a particularly "complicated case in New York," where Ms. Jenkins spends a fair amount of time with a variety of corporate clients, thus allowing the two to enjoy occasional weekends together. While at first Ms. Jenkins enjoyed the relationship for the sex and easy companionship, she now finds herself in love.

Mr. Robertson claims to be smitten as well, and has complained bitterly about his sexless marriage. He has told Ms. Jenkins that he "wishes he could leave his wife and marry Ms. Jenkins." And, if it weren't for his two boys, he would have left her long ago. When she asks if he might leave when his sons are older, he says "only if you're there waiting." Ms. Jenkins, who tends to be very pragmatic, accepts this explanation as reasonable, offering him a sympathetic ear. She claims to respect his predicament and has promised to be patient until he leaves his wife. But, over the last year, she's started to worry whether she's wasting her time. All of the talk about family and children has made her concerned Mr. Robertson will not want to start a new family with her irrespective of his potential availability.

DATE SCENE RECONSTRUCTION

Two Months into Affair: Afternoon Despite

LOCALE: Best Western, Malden, MA

Synopsis: Led to assume she was being taken out for a romantic seaside lunch, Mr. Robertson instead took her to a drive-through McDonald's and a nearby motel featuring free XXX-rated videos, overhead mirrors, and a vibrating bed. While Ms. Jenkins was always eager to make love with Mr. Robertson, she had hoped for something a bit less tawdry. Mr. Robertson claimed the harborside restaurant was too risky, so he'd chosen a fast-food joint and a nearby motel so they would have the most time alone together. He promised her the next time would be better.

Witness Testimony: The motel manager, who sees his fair share of hourly guests, noted that Ms. Jenkins seemed disappointed with the quality of the room and inquired about the fiber content of the sheets: "So I says to her, 'I don't feed my pillows no bran muffins, missy.'" A member of the housekeeping staff noted that Mr. Robertson seemed anxious and hurried her into the room while covering his face with the *Wall Street Journal* "as if he was a fugitive of the law!"

Four Months into Affair: Cabin Fever

LOCALE: Malibu, CA

Synopsis: When Ms. Jenkins was assigned a client in Silicon Valley, Mr. Robertson took the opportunity to make a recruiting expedition to some of the California law schools for summer associates. The couple then spent a weekend together at a small bed-and-breakfast in Malibu. While the setting was spectacular, as their cottage boasted a private trail to the rocky tides, their activities remained strictly relegated to the bedroom, despite Ms. Jenkins' pleas to take a midnight stroll on the beach.

Witness Testimony: According to the owner of the B&B, Mr. Robertson was constantly on his cell phone and seemed to be arguing with someone all the time about missing some kid's sporting event. "We have a real nice bistro on the premises and a free breakfast buffet in a gazebo overlooking the ocean, which all the ladies go ga-ga for, but he just kept on ordering up grilled cheese and French fries from room service."

Six Months into Affair: The Graduate

LOCALE: Graduation party for eldest child, Mr. Robertson's home, Brookline, MA

Synopsis: In an effort to conceal his affair by demonstrating his platonic friendship with Ms. Jenkins, Mr. Robertson invited her to a graduation party at his home. While she had mixed feelings about this plan, her desire and curiosity won out. Upon arriving at the party, she was introduced as a work associate, and nobody, including Mr. Robertson's wife, an attractive, well-put-together older woman, thought much about it. Ms. Jenkins became overcome with jealousy when she saw Mr. Robertson touch his wife's shoulder and hand her a drink, surrounded by hundreds of family photos, so much so that she left the party without saying goodbye.

Witness Testimony: Bob, the bartender, tried to cheer up the "sullen but beautiful young woman" without success, and ended up serving her at least seven white-wine spritzers. A waitress claims she saw Ms. Jenkins giving Mr. Robertson's wife the evil eye, and even heard her mutter the words "skinny old bitch" under her breath.

FORENSIC ASSESSMENT AND EVIDENTIARY ANALYSIS

Physical Evidence

A DSI investigation into Mr. Robertson's personal and financial affairs showed no evidence that suggested that Mr. Robertson was preparing to leave his family. In fact, the evidence seemed to reveal the opposite:

- The recent purchase of a diamond anniversary bracelet for his wife, celebrating twenty years of marriage

- Joint ownership of two homes, including a second beach home purchased during the time of his relationship with Ms. Jenkins

- Joint checking accounts and the creation of several trusts in his wife's name

- Recent gifts of French lingerie to his wife, which were dry-cleaned the day after purchase

- Discussions of family vacations spanning the next four years, including a pre-purchased rental of a Tuscan Villa for the following summer

A sweep of Ms. Jenkins' dwelling space and her computer records indicated that Mr. Robertson had, indeed, led her to believe he was preparing to leave his wife:

→ A Tiffany watch was found, engraved with the words "my true love"

→ Numerous cards and notes were similarly signed and included such phrases as "You are the love of my life," "I want to grow old with you," and "I am yours now and forever."

→ Emails were saved detailing Mr. Robertson's unhappiness at home along with the following oft-repeated desire: "I want to marry you and make you mine forever."

→ Several sexy and romantic photographs of their weekend trysts were framed and hung on Ms. Jenkins' wall, indicating that Mr. Robertson was her exclusive male partner

→ A copy of *Stepmotherhood: How to Survive Without Feeling Frustrated, Left Out, or Wicked* was on her bookshelf

Forensic Metrics

Divorce Evaluation Not In A Lifetime (DENIAL) Test

Utilizing the DENIAL Test, which determines the likelihood that a married cheating husband will leave his current wife, DSI determined that Mr. Robertson scored well below average, indicating a strong improbability of imminent separation or dissolution. Every barometer assessed—emotional, economic, and parental responsibility—fell well below threshold, consistent with the profile of the classic cheating husband who will never rock the boat.

Self-Aware and Normally Emotional (SANE) Analysis

Given Ms. Jenkins' seemingly high levels of self-deception in this case, DSI undertook a SANE analysis. This analysis examines a person's emotional and psychological states to determine his or her level of emotional intelligence. It was determined that while Ms. Jenkins had potential ability in this area, her current emotional IQ placed her at the level of a chimp raised in captivity. Further testing revealed that the blockage stemmed from her own inability to commit.

DSI FINDING

Based on all available evidence, Ms. Jenkins is clearly suffering from Mistress Madness. As a secondary finding, we determine that Mr. Robertson is highly unlikely to terminate his marriage. This assessment is deemed secondary in that it is unclear whether Ms. Jenkins and Mr. Robertson established a deeper emotional bond sufficient to sustain a long-term relationship, notwithstanding his unavailability.

RELATIONSHIP REHAB

Given the extreme nature of Ms. Jenkins' Mistress Madness condition, and the very low probability that Mr. Robertson would ever leave his wife, DSI determined the following course of action:

- Ms. Jenkins must end the relationship at once.

- Ms. Jenkins should begin counseling to overcome her resistance to intimacy and to help her understand and improve her romantic object choices.

- Ms. Jenkins should undertake cognitive-therapy exercises to help her realize that even if Mr. Robertson did get divorced, her dreams for a relationship would never have materialized based on broader incompatibility.

- Ms. Jenkins must come clean with her family and friends and create a support system to help her work through the period of mourning and start fresh.

➤ Ms. Jenkins should start a new exercise routine and buy some new clothes for her new single life.

➤ Mr. Robertson should figure out how to make his marriage more intimate and passionate, so he isn't driven to seek fulfillment outside the relationship.

In lieu of Rehab, DSI undertook an Intimacy Intervention, dispatching field agents to assist Ms. Jenkins in a complete removal of Mr. Robertson from her life (including all totems and reminders). Team DSI monitored progress through regular MRI scans of brain patterns. Consistent with those in love, we found high level of activity in areas of the brain associated with emotional attachment, indicating that she was suffering from a profound sense of mourning. While the withdrawal period was difficult, the DSI Intimacy Intervention was successful, and Ms. Jenkins was finally able to see things from a more lucid perspective and move on.

DATING DIAGNOSTIC

Let's put it this way: we all get lazy. Sometimes we'd rather eat our roommate's leftovers than go out and prepare a meal of our own. Still, many of us make a good faith effort to eat right, but occasionally slip up when the temptation is simply too great to resist. But what about those of us who want *only* what we can't have? If we're on a low-carb diet, we are helpless to the lure of chocolate mousse and BBQ potato chips. Sure, it may not be healthy for us, but sooner or later, we give in. And man, does it taste good.

Those of us who have been there before know better than to judge without regard to circumstance. Perhaps we didn't know he or she was involved with someone else. Or, maybe we did know, but decided it was their moral tally to reckon, not ours, and what we wanted did not encroach upon what they had at home anyway. Or, perhaps we fell in love. We never meant for it to happen and would not have chosen it deliberately, but nonetheless we gave in to the bittersweet taste of romance. Yet for a number of us, sleeping with married people becomes a nasty habit, one that is hard to quit. The stolen moments, the clandestine passion, the joy of frolicking in someone else's garden. The question is: what happens next?

Mistress Madness takes many shapes and forms. In some cases, the mistress is fully aware that she is, simply put, "the other woman," and the arrangement may work to her advantage, since she does not want anything more than a no-strings-attached dynamic. Women who are commitment-phobic often favor this type of scenario, since they can enjoy the intimacy and passion of a relationship without a long-term commitment. Even so, the finite nature, power inequity, and lack of companionship generally lead to conflict, resentment, and depression.

In most cases, however, the mistress invests serious emotional stock in the viability of the relationship, marked by a strong sense of hope for a future together. Some women feel they can "win" the cheating husband over by offering an irresistible sanctuary from the stressful tedium of marriage. In most cases, however, the mistress ends up waiting around for years, only to realize that she's been wasting her time. This often leads to a "crisis in rationalization," in which it is no longer possible to justify the situation, followed by desperate behavior and an uncontrollable impulse to break the tacit rules of engagement, including late-night phone calls, unreasonable demands for time, ultimatums, and other "boiled bunnies" of fatal attraction.

Yet despite all the negatives, recidivism is strong. Affairs between single women and married men are often very passionate—weekend getaways, secret trysts at motels, stolen kisses in the office supply closet, the thrill of being the sultry seductress he simply can't resist. The sex is spontaneous, dangerous, and in the moment, and there is very little everyday life to get in the way: no arguments over balancing checkbooks, private versus public schooling, or whether it's leftover chicken or pizza for dinner, again.

For women who have busy careers and a hunger for hot encounters without obligation, married men can become addictive. But even when deeper emotions develop and the husband decides to leave his wife, generally for reasons that have nothing to do with the affair (despite the misogynist "home-wrecker" epithet), long-term lovers may find they lack a foundation of daily familiarity. So much of an affair is devoted to pragmatics (e.g., when will I see you, where, how, what about the time after?) that little energy is leftover for other activities, such as hobbies, conversation, and simple routine. As a result, when the obstacles to a relationship are finally overcome, couples may be in for a rude awakening to discover their seemingly perfect fantasy partner is just a regular guy with all the associated foibles attached.

FOLLOW-UP

After DSI apprehended Mr. Robertson and Ms. Jenkins for engaging in an emotionally damaging relationship, Ms. Jenkins succeeded in making a clean break, entailing a serious period of withdrawal (marked by incessantly checking email and voicemail hoping Mr. Robertson would not honor her "no-contact" request). Following up on DSI's suggestions, Ms. Jenkins purchased some sexy outfits, resumed yoga, and started going out more regularly with her single friends, and she soon found herself enjoying her single status. Her recent dating efforts have shown progress in that none of the men have been married and two were several years her junior. While she admits to having "a thing for nooners in sleazy motels," she intends to incorporate that preference into her next relationship.

DO YOU SUFFER FROM MISTRESS MADNESS SYNDROME (MMS)?

If you answer yes to seven or more of the following questions, consider yourself guilty as charged:

1. When you discover a man is married, does your interest wax rather than wane?

2. In the past, have you gotten bored once the newness of a relationship wears thin?

3. Do you fantasize about him choosing you over his wife without imagining what it would be like to set up house with him and help raise his/your kids?

4. Would you be unable to answer most of the following: (a) his favorite author; (b) his favorite old movie; (c) his favorite columnist; (d) his favorite thing to do on a rainy day; (d) his favorite old sit-com; (e) his favorite tie?

5. Does the idea of having sex with him as your husband seem less arousing than as his mistress?

6. Do you frequently fantasize about getting caught in the act together?

7. Do you take pride in the fact that he finds you sexier than his wife?

8. Are your dates mainly focused around sex (at the expense of normal dating activities and romance)?

9. Are you hurt that you do not socialize with his friends? Have you asked to meet them and been rebuffed?

10. Do you collude with your lover in blaming his wife for the affair, alleging it is owing to her low sex drive or other unresolved emotional issues?

11. Do you often claim that all the good men are taken and you had no other choice?

12. Do you believe you don't have time for a "regular" relationship because of your career or other priorities?

COMMON ARSE EXCUSES FOR AVOIDING COMMITMENT

A DSI Study

The Federal Bureau of Intimacy is proud to release the results of a long-term classified study of Male Anti-Relationship Syndrome (MARS, hence substantiating the idiom that men are, indeed, from Mars). The unearthing of these documents has helped shed new light on a variety of male dating behaviors once thought to be beyond comprehension. Below we present an unedited and unabridged transcript of an interrogation with a typical ARSE.

File Name: I'm Just Not Ready for a Serious Relationship
Date of Interrogation: May 25, 2005
ARSE Profile: Robert Conrad
Age: 34
Location: Baltimore, MD
Occupation: Landscape architect
DSI Disorder: Fear of Commitment

Circumstances of Interrogation

Following an anonymous tip, DSI field agents apprehended Mr. Conrad at his gym, pursuant to several corroborating reports implicating his involvement in a serious relationship infraction plagued by an untreated fear of commitment. According to our records, Mr. Conrad is a repeat offender, having tendered as the sole explanation for six consecutive break-ups that he had "too much other shit going on" and was "not yet ready to make a long-term commitment."

Interrogation Transcript

DSI: So, have anything to say for yourself, Conrad, before we begin questioning?

ARSE: I have nothing to hide. I was honest with Marla and the others about what I want.

DSI: So it's a coincidence that all six of your previous girlfriends developed the same misimpression about your interest in engaging in a committed relationship?

ARSE: It's not my fault they all chose to read too much into what I may have said in the heat of the moment. Look, I'm innocent. I know my rights. You guys don't have anything on me.

DSI: Oh no? What's this then? [The DSI agent produced a handwritten letter from the ARSE to one of his ex-girlfriends.]

ARSE: That? I have no idea.

DSI: This is a letter you wrote to one Janice Fishberg. Remember her? The girl whose heart you broke after eight months of dating, telling her, and I quote, "I can see spending the rest of my life with you." Then you ditched her like yesterday's tuna surprise when she indicated that the sentiment was reciprocated. According to our files, you broke up with her via email, stating, "I care about you far too much to make you suffer through my own indecision as I figure out what I want out of life and out of the relationship; speaking of which, I want out of the relationship. Best always, Bob." Then when she expressed a willingness to help you sort through those issues, you failed to reply and subsequently blocked her from your email account.

ARSE: Look, first off, I meant what I said. I did have genuine feelings for the girl, but I was going through some serious shit at the time, like about whether I wanted to go into commercial landscaping or stick with residential. The timing just wasn't right. And I could tell she was starting to have, you know, serious expectations. I couldn't lead her on like that. I did it for her own good.

DSI: You have broken up with the last six women via email with the same lame excuse that you're "not ready" and have "other shit going on" and don't want to subject them to your "indecision." If that's the case, why do you keep on going back for more?

ARSE: I'm ready to date. I'm just not ready to commit to dating.

DSI: You can't or you won't?

ARSE: I'm just not ready for that level of commitment.

DSI: See, that's where I disagree with you, Conrad. Because you're able to commit to your job.

ARSE: Well . . .

DSI: And you're able to commit to the football and baseball games you follow so religiously, often to the exclusion of the women in your life.

ARSE: So what?

DSI: Well, genius, all of those examples demonstrate some capacity to focus and to be committed to something. So I'm just wondering how you can say you're "not ready" for a relationship.

ARSE: I guess I'm just not ready to settle down yet. Is that a crime?

DSI: No, it's not. But leading them on and then dumping them for expecting something you've made them think possible—that is a crime here at DSI.

ARSE: You can't make me commit if I don't want to. I'm not ready to get nailed in the coffin yet. This is America, and I choose freedom!

DSI: Well, then, you'll have all the freedom you want, because you've been declared a national dating disaster zone. There won't be anybody treading on your turf until you make some serious changes to improve the hazardous conditions.

ARSE: And how am I supposed to do that?

DSI: By spending the next twelve months thinking about everything you're not getting.

ARSE: Wait, do you mean, no women?

DSI: That's right, Mr. Conrad. Rest assured, you'll have nobody clamoring for your love and affection. So, enjoy your freedom. You earned it.

FIVE:
COLD SHEET FILES

THE CASE OF THE COUPLE WHOSE SEX LIFE
SUCKED (CUZ HE DIDN'T)

THE DSI 911

DSI received a call from an agitated complainant named Genine Kessler. Ms. Kessler was confused about an alleged sexual issue, reporting that she didn't know what to do about her boyfriend's lack of reciprocation in "certain areas." She didn't want to make him feel defensive or force him to do something he found unappealing, but certain aspects of their sex life (or lack thereof) were leaving her cold. Stated Kessler: "He never goes down on me, but expects me to do him all the time. Anytime I tell him how much I'd love for him to, ya know, dive down and swim a few laps, he gets flustered and says I'm ruining the moment. Then he tells me how his previous girlfriend got so turned on sucking him that she had multiple orgasms just from rubbing her own nipples! I've been alone for too long to let an argument over sex ruin the relationship. On the other hand, I'm getting seriously pissed off waiting for him to roll over and fall asleep so I can take the old bunny for a hop. I mean, I thought once I had a serious boyfriend I wouldn't have to buy batteries so often. But now, I'm so frustrated, I'm like going through a pack a week."

PRELIMINARY DIAGNOSIS

The preliminary DSI diagnosis suggests severe Cunnilingus Antagonist Disorder (CAD) coupled with a lack of understanding of basic female anatomy. Left untreated, these disorders can lead "normal" women to give their shower massagers pet names and/or renounce sex altogether to devote more quality time to compiling nonstimulating iPod playlists featuring Barry Manilow and Celine Dion.

PARALLEL CASE ANECDOTALS

"After six months of faking it, I tried to talk to my boyfriend about his reluctance to go down on me. He got really mad and shouted, 'What's the big deal? It's not like you're not having orgasms anyway!' I didn't know what to say—at that point I was in too deep."

—Pauline, 32

"For me, it's not about the orgasms, but about the lack of connection that accompanies bad sex. But men get so wrapped up in their abilities and their prowess that it's impossible to talk about it."

—Marybeth, 26

"I'm not about to risk blowing a relationship over sex. I have bigger goals: marriage, children—a partner in life. I guess I can put up with someone so-so between the sheets."

—Kim, 34

"When I found out my girlfriend of two years had been faking it the whole time, it blew me away. I couldn't even look at her—why didn't she just tell me in the beginning what wasn't working?"

—Ronald, 31

CASE SPECIFICS

The Dupe: Genine Kessler
Age: 34
Location: Los Angeles, CA
Occupation: Freelance journalist
Hair: Brown
Eyes: Blue
Height: 5'2"
Weight: 102

RELATIONSHIP RAP SHEET/EX FILES

Past Serious Relationships: 6
Total Number of Sexual Partners: 17
Exes Still in Contact: 2

Interpersonal Infractions

→ History of being intensely marriage-oriented, something she considers a primary goal

→ Often sacrifices her own feelings to keep a failing relationship alive

→ Has a pattern of dating men she knows are wrong for her, lowering her standards to adjust to the grim reality of the competitive dating market

Mating Misdemeanors

June 2003

During a long beach weekend with a man she had just started dating, Ms. Kessler began interrogating him about the interior design plans for his country home, and seemed to be making suggestions that were for the both of them. The man broke up with her the next week.

Flirtatious Felonies

April 1999

While dating a man ten years her senior during her first reporting job, she continually let his bad behavior and inappropriate chasing of other women slide, believing that it was more an indication of his age than his attitude or feelings for her.

October 2002

Cheated on a live-in boyfriend with a mutual friend after the boyfriend recited the "I'm not ready for a serious commitment" speech, to which she tearfully replied, "Well, it's all your fault that I had to fake orgasms for the last two years and go unsatisfied. God forbid you get your puny fingers wet. At least Scott asks me if I've come instead of just assuming it after three minutes of pathetic poking and panting. And, oh yeah, Scott didn't tell me he's not ready to commit after I wasted two precious years of my life on him either, you lame-assed, small-dicked *loser!*"

Psychographic Thumbnail

Ms. Kessler has a strong history of wanting to get married and have children, along with a detailed timeline of when she intends to have her first son, second daughter, and four grandchildren (two boys and two girls). The intensity of this desire has led her to lower her standards, especially now that her original timeline has expired. Some of the pressure comes from her Midwestern parents, who always told her that marriage is the most important thing in a woman's life. Her friends, primarily single professionals like herself, have similarly found themselves compromising their standards in recent years. While the group formerly did a fair amount of clubbing and casual dating, even the most sexually adventurous among them has grown wary that her "prime years" are running out. Their constant discussion about the lack of marriageable men has only exacerbated her anxieties, causing her to dip the bar ever lower in the search for Mr. Eh.

"For better or for worse," however, Ms. Kessler remains a hopeless romantic with a hearty sexual appetite. While she has been willing to compromise on other bright-line issues concerning synergy of interests and professional/financial dossier, she finds it challenging to have sex with a man she is not in love with, especially if he is "a total dweeb in bed." Based on her perceived need to go out with guys who are "way beneath" her, she has developed a sense of injured entitlement, which has cast a cynical cloud over her view of sexual relations. With that has come a fatalistic determinism that she will "never be sexually fulfilled or in love." Faking it seems a small price to pay for a Malibu beach house and a family, thus Kessler attempts to keep her frustrations in check . . . *most of the time.*

The Arse: William Silverstein
Age: 36
Location: Los Angeles, CA
Occupation: Television executive
Hair: Brown
Eyes: Brown
Height: 5'10"
Weight: 180

RELATIONSHIP RAP SHEET/EX FILES

Past Serious Relationships: 6
Total Number of Sexual Partners: 19
Exes Still in Contact: 5

Interpersonal Infractions

→ Often accused of being a poor listener and self-absorbed.

→ Has difficulty acknowledging the professional accomplishments of women he dates.

→ Will not engage in sexual activity with a woman unless she's as "smooth as a baby's bottom."

→ Refuses to let Ms. Kessler leave tampons in his medicine cabinet, since he finds them vulgar and unappealing. Though Mr. Silverstein is unwilling to touch Ms. Kessler or watch her touch herself through double layers of clothing when she is menstruating, he believes the least she can do is perform oral sex on him during her "special time."

→ Says he is "willing to go down only upon special request," but admits to finding cunnilingus "a smelly turn-off, especially if the woman gets too excited."

→ Will only ejaculate on Ms. Kessler's breasts or face, even after intercourse, and further states that if she does not make eye contact during such time, "it totally kills the fun."

→ Overtly ogles women with breast implants, yet calls them "dirty skanks," frequently lamenting the fact that Ms. Kessler is so small-breasted.

→ Grades every woman he meets on a scale of 1 to 10 (rating Ms. Kessler in the 7 range), with 10 being Pamela Anderson and 1 being any woman who reminds him of his mother.

→ Likes to remark at parties that his choice of Ms. Kessler as a long-term partner proves he is not superficial.

Mating Misdemeanors

October 2000

Asked his girlfriend of nine months to throw him a surprise birthday party and then broke up with her the day after the party to date one of her (former) best friends, whom he met at said party.

Known for being the "go-to-go-go-guy" when it comes to arranging "quality" bachelor parties, Mr. Silverstein only hires strippers under the age of twenty-five with 38DD breasts or larger who are willing to do one-on-ones wearing whipped cream bikinis while he takes pictures. He makes a point of inviting his father, a successful Hollywood agent, to all such engagements, since he likes to see the old man "have a good time." When a girlfriend of his asked that he not partake in a lap dance or other tactile encounter at one such party, he said, "Are you kidding? They give me a free kickback, if you catch my drift."

Flirtatious Felonies

February 1995–May 1997
Dated a college film professor who boosted his GPA, among other things, and supported him throughout graduate school. After he finished with high honors due to the "blazingly innovative" short films she wrote and produced for him, she recommended him for a coveted film production job in LA, offering to take a nontenured teaching position at UCLA and go with him (although she was already tenured at NYU). Mr. Silverstein broke up with her a week after he signed his employment contract, leaving her with a pound of salted cashews (his favorite) and the immortal words, "See you at the movies."

Psychographic Thumbnail

Mr. Silverstein is what most women would call a selfish, self-centered bastard. An only child, he is often oblivious to the needs of others and possesses a strong sense of being special. This leads him to engage in bawdy behavior or make statements for their shock value to remain at the center of attention at all times. In relationships with women, he puts his professional, personal, and sexual needs above theirs and has a difficult time empathizing with their "little issues." He claims he wants to get married and have a family, and sees Ms. Kessler as an excellent candidate, since she is relatively low-maintenance and appears to have a fast metabolism and is therefore unlikely to "blimp out after popping them out." A charismatic extrovert, he is capable of being incredibly charming, funny, and generous and considers himself a "real catch." What he likes best about Ms. Kessler is her "old-fashioned" values and apparent adoration of him.

During foreplay, he enjoys taunting her on a regular basis by saying how "bad" he knows "she wants it" and demanding that she say "please" before he penetrates her. This behavior is consistent with the reports of prior ex-partners, one of whom stated, "He seemed to think it turned me on to beg for it, as he put it. And he always made this big announcement before he came on my boobs about how desperate I was to get it. I was like, oh whatever, can you just grab some paper towels so we can go to dinner already?"

RELATIONSHIP RECONNAISSANCE

Ms. Kessler and Mr. Silverstein met the way many couples do in Los Angeles, at a movie premiere. They'd actually "met" several years before, on a blind date set up by mutual friends, but both were dating other people at the time, so nothing happened. This made their second meeting a nice surprise (although Mr. Silverstein failed to recognize Ms. Kessler until she reminded him that they'd gone out before). Mr. Silverstein was very charming from the get-go. Their first date involved a romantic drive up the California Coast, followed by a dinner in Malibu, and then a night of sex. While Ms. Kessler did not generally sleep with men on the first date, she felt like she already knew Mr. Silverstein and that it just "felt right." Despite seeing herself as a modern woman, Ms. Kessler fretted afterward that Mr. Silverstein might not call again. He did, however, two days later and soon they were seriously dating. The mutual friend who originally set them up bumped into Ms. Kessler at Starbucks and teased her about having "kinky sex with Jonny on the first night," which Ms. Kessler thought showed very bad taste on Mr. Silverstein's part. But by that point, they'd been dating for two months and things seemed to be going fairly well.

In terms of their sex life, there is a high degree of dissatisfaction on Ms. Kessler's part, although Mr. Silverstein had no complaints, nor he is aware of Ms. Kessler's discontent. She has largely faked orgasm due to his unwillingness to provide direct clitoral stimulation of any sort, which he finds "unsexy." When she attempted various times to stroke herself during intercourse or while performing oral sex on him, he moved her hand away and scolded: "You naughty girl. You're going to have to wait until I'm good and ready." After a particularly close call when she was "riding [him] like a dirty cowgirl," he pulled out right before he was about to come to thrust himself into her mouth, causing her to holler, "Next time, you're going to go down on me, buddy." His response, later, was, "What's the big deal? You always come, no matter what I do. That's what I love about you!" It was the first time Mr. Silverstein told Ms. Kessler that he loved her. Her excitement led her to exclaim, "That's true. Why was I being so silly?" While Ms. Kessler was not in love with Mr. Silverstein and resented his willful ignorance of female sexuality, she was still delighted. After all, he was a handsome, smart, successful LA film producer who said he wanted marriage and children. So what if she had to do herself in the shower after he fell asleep? He just said he loved her!! Sort of.

DATE SCENE RECONSTRUCTION

Three Months into Dating: Sex, Lies on Videotape

LOCALE: Mr. Silverstein's bedroom

Synopsis: Following another brief, unsatisfying (for her) sex session, Mr. Silverstein rolled over and turned on *The Daily Show*, without bothering to inquire whether Ms. Kessler had had her fill. Upset and still aroused, Ms. Kessler turned off the TV, grabbed Mr. Silverstein's hand and began masturbating herself with his clenched fingers and the remote control. "Babe, I'm sorry, I'm just tired," protested Mr. Silverstein, who pulled away and turned on the TV (instead of Ms. Kessler). "Would you like to watch me?" asked Ms. Kessler, hoping to rouse him into a more compliant student. "You already came. Enough already," he retorted. Upset, and still aroused, Ms. Kessler grabbed the remote, turned off the television and launched into a tirade: "You need to think with your tongue, buddy," she said. "Or you're going to wind up using that hand of yours an awful lot." When Mr. Silverstein tried to defend himself by saying that she'd had an orgasm, she retorted that her climax was "as real as the Easter Bunny," and then proceeded to masturbate in front of him with her vibrating cell phone. The couple then went to bed, ignoring the issues that had been raised.

Witness Testimony: An older woman who lives in the adjoining apartment, who overheard the entire exchange, said, "Do you happen to know where she bought that cell phone and if Verizon supports it?"

Eight Months into Dating: Porn to Run

LOCALE: Bungalow 4, The Bay Inn, St. Maarten

Synopsis: After eight months of serious dating, Mr. Silverstein whisked Ms. Kessler off to a secluded oceanfront cabin in a lush tropical paradise, where there was nothing to distract them from each other but the whir of morning crickets and the lap of frothy tides. Convinced Mr. Silverstein was gearing up to pop the question, Ms. Kessler brought her finest selection of French lingerie and had even *boned up* on some new techniques she'd learned from a porn-star how-to guide by practicing on a lucky zucchini. But when they got to the rustic retreat scented with bowls of fresh coconut, mango, and papaya, the first thing Mr. Silverstein did was to collapse onto the swinging bamboo hammock and unzip his fly. "Ready for your afternoon cocktail, baby?" Whereupon, Mr. Silverstein proudly retrieved his favorite toy, threw a pillow on the floor, and pointed. For the next three days, Ms. Kessler remained the only person in a ten-mile radius to fall on bended knee. Still believing he was getting ready to propose, however, she endured a full roster of porn classics, including up against the wall, doggy-style, between the breasts, the buttocks, and dirty on the beach. While Ms. Kessler made a concerted effort to move Mr. Silverstein's hand between her thighs while he was taking her from behind, he said "Hey, you're making me lose my balance." And when she attempted to do it herself, he said, "There'll be plenty of time for that, you dirty girl." Mr. Silverstein never did get around to touching her, proposing, or even taking a much-talked-about romantic stroll by the dunes. While Mr. Silverstein deserves some credit for trying to spice things up, the scenario underscores his lack of sensitivity and the couple's poor communication.

Witness Testimony: A customs agent who inspected Mr. Silverstein's bag on the way back into the United States noted that he had "more Viagra than a pharmacy" in his carry-on luggage, and that Ms. Kessler appeared to be limping.

Five Months into Dating: The Eyes Have It

LOCALE: Ms. Kessler's bedroom

Synopsis: Following a particularly stressful workweek for Mr. Silverstein, who had just pitched a multimillion dollar movie deal and was waiting to hear the verdict, the couple went to a dinner party and back to Ms. Kessler's place. Wanting to give him a special treat, she put on a sexy new peignoir and gave him a hot oil massage. Mr. Silverstein was tired, but enthusiastic. Too enthusiastic, in fact: he suffered his first bout of premature ejaculation (or so he claimed). Feeling ashamed after Ms. Kessler had gone to so much trouble, he apologized. And the couple genuinely connected, nuzzling each other softly to sleep. In the morning, Mr. Silverstein again thanked Ms. Kessler for her understanding, still laboring under the delusion that his "failure to perform" the night before had proven a grave disappointment. While he did not go down on her, he stroked her tenderly before he entered her and they made love in plain old missionary style, making eye contact the whole time. It was one of the few moments that she saw him show some sign of vulnerability.

Witness Testimony: Mr. Silverstein's assistant reported that he was "unnaturally relaxed and pleasant" the next morning, and that he'd only snapped at her twice the whole day, even though he still hadn't heard if he'd landed "that idiot movie deal."

FORENSIC ASSESSMENT AND EVIDENTIARY ANALYSIS

DSI's preliminary assessment indicates that Mr. Silverstein suffers from deep-seated misogyny and disgust of female genitalia, which is difficult, if not impossible, to reprogram into positive desire. At best, Mr. Silverstein could be reeducated to understand the centrality of the clitoris to female orgasm and the fact that, despite what he's seen in strip clubs and porn, the thrusting of a penis in a woman's face does not necessarily incite begging or induce orgasmic frenzy.

Physical Evidence

A survey of Ms. Kessler's home revealed that while she is very sexually open, she is also confused about how to express this freedom. Our search revealed the following:

- An entire bedside drawer devoted to sex toys, including several vibrators, handcuffs, lube, and a paddle
- Half a bookshelf in her living room devoted to vintage and contemporary erotica
- A standing monthly appointment for a Brazilian bikini wax
- Several books on how to give the perfect blow job and where to meet the perfect husband
- A scrapbook devoted to "dream weddings," an Internet bookmark to TheKnot.com, and several copies of well-thumbed wedding dress catalogues

Our investigation of Mr. Silverstein's dwelling revealed:

→ An assortment of porn tapes and magazines, covering a variety of mainstream themes, such as "girl-on-girl," facials, and things to do with/on unhealthily large silicone implants

→ A noticeable preponderance of photos and old sporting trophies bearing Mr. Silverstein's name or semblance, without a single photo in which Mr. Silverstein does not appear in a flattering pose

→ A large shelf of hardcover classics that appear to be in their original cellophane wrappers

→ A mirror on the bedroom wall and a digital video camera on the nightstand

Forensic Metrics

Sexual Potential And Romantic Kinship (SPARK) Test

A SPARK test was administered to the couple by DSI, which measures the level of sexual chemistry between two people. The SPARK reading between Ms. Kessler and Mr. Silverstein was very warm, indicating that they had the potential for passionate intimacy and great sex. The results led DSI to conclude that what had been missing from their sex life, more than rudimentary reciprocity, was a deeper, more emotional connection. The lab results pointed to only one conclusion (at least on paper): these two people should be having incredibly hot sex.

Clitoral Literacy Impairment Test (CLIT)

An infrared camera installed in both of the relevant bedrooms revealed that Mr. Silverstein suffers from a severe case of ill-cliteracy. In other words, he lacks a basic understanding of, and appreciation for, female anatomy and sexual pleasuring. Whether it is owing to ignorance, accident, or intentional denial, Mr. Silverstein's ill-cliteracy rate is off the charts. The CLIT also indicated symptoms of chronic premature ejaculation, which he compensated for with steady dosage of Viagra and by fixating on his porn-style performance-centric repertoire of positions. The confluence of these factors explains how a couple with such a high SPARK reading could have such a bad sex life.

Intimate Communications Evaluation (ICE)

Ms. Kessler and Mr. Silverstein had fallen into traditional sex scripts, a breezy shorthand that leads couples to miss out on honest communications and mutual understanding. Ms. Kessler was afraid to openly discuss her hopes for marriage and children and her desires for a more passionate and fulfilling sex life, while Mr. Silverstein's anxieties about his sexual performance led him to replicate pornographic imagery to ensure he was "doing things right." His chronic fears of sexual inadequacy kept him from focusing on her pleasure, so worried was he about being found a sexual imposter or failure. Ironically, it was this very sense of failure that ultimately liberated Mr. Silverstein and allowed him to see that there was life after premature ejaculation and love after, and even during, sex.

DSI FINDING

DSI concludes that while Mr. Silverstein suffers from willful ignorance of female sexuality and self-absorbed insensitivity to others' needs, the etiology of his condition indicates chronic fears of failure rather than reckless disregard of feelings, which means there is hope. Ms. Kessler was likewise culpable for letting her fears of losing a prospective husband undermine her honesty about what she wanted and expected, both in and out of bed. It remains unclear whether the couple will have enough in common to support a long-term relationship at this time.

RELATIONSHIP REHAB

In order for this relationship to work, DSI has identified the following long- and short-term goals:

→ Ms. Kessler must learn to express her sexual needs in a manner that is not unduly critical of Mr. Silverstein.

→ Ms. Kessler must stop faking orgasms and understand that her pleasure should be a mutual objective.

→ Rather than pressuring Mr. Silverstein to go down on her, she must find ways to respond to his fears rationally and constructively (for instance, let him wash her if he is phobic about hygiene).

→ She needs to separate her desire for marriage and children from her choice of Mr. Silverstein in order to assess whether the two (goals and people) are compatible.

→ She also needs to stop feeling anger/resentment for the choices she's making. If she is with someone she knows is not right for her, she should end the relationship or accept the limitations of the arrangement.

→ Mr. Silverstein must focus on developing a healthier, more realistic knowledge and understanding of women's physiology and sexuality; DSI further recommends a ban on porn until further notice.

→ Mr. Silverstein must find ways to satisfy Ms. Kessler's desires that are not centered on his sexual performance.

→ Both parties must continue to strengthen their emotional connection in and out of bed.

DATING DIAGNOSTIC

One of the most common questions DSI receives from women, day after day, year after year, remains strangely unchanged: "how can I learn to have orgasms while my boyfriend is making love to me?" Implicit in this question is, "what's wrong with me?" In fact, the problem is not the failure to achieve orgasm during intercourse, but the continuing myth that such an occurrence is likely or necessarily desirable. But this internalization of guilt and complicity is the beginning of a vicious cycle that drives perfectly smart, healthy, orgasmic women to fake it in order to meet some illusory ideal perpetuated by cultural idioms (primarily pornography) which in turn reinforce the erroneous view that "really sexy women" climax during intercourse without clitoral stimulation.

That said, communicating about sex is often touchy, and many women make the mistake of expressing their concerns in the heat of the moment or adopting an accusatory tone to compensate for their feelings of failure. That only makes a bad situation worse, causing their partners to withdraw and get defensive. To resolve the issue, they often fake it the next time, compounding the miscommunication, ignorance, and resentment.

Let's face it: we live in an uptight, sex-crazed culture that force-feeds us plastic, super-sized myths of what sex is supposed to look like from the outside looking in. The problem is we don't live on the outside looking in. We live on the inside out: we are messy bundles of flesh and neuroses that do not transmogrify into ravishing sex-starved dream-bots from the moment our partners stroll through the door. And our partners, for that matter, do not typically heave us to the floor in a fit of unbridled passion and make love to us without mussing our hair.

But when we turn on our TVs and computers, we see instant sex without daily burdens. We see tight bodies absent of annoying personal tics, large-breasted women who have not yet disappointed us, muscular men who have not forgotten our birthdays or left their dirty clothes under the kitchen table. And, frankly, those digital hotties get a little dull, too, after a while. We tire of their particular brand of perfection and crave a slightly newer version.

It's important to remind ourselves that while media images suggest that everybody is having tons of great sex without even trying, keeping the passion fresh beyond the first throes of romance requires a lot of hard work. All too often, people are ready to write off the other person simply because the sex isn't what it once was or maybe ever was. But without an expert stage crew doing makeup, lighting, and a fair amount of fluffing on the sidelines, even porn stars don't have XXX sex.

That kind of wake-up-the-neighbors sex demands more than good technique and generous assets, it requires both partners to know what their lover truly wants by screening out the rest of the world and becoming singularly attuned to the person in their bed (or shower or pickup truck) and opening themselves up to candid communication and intimacy.

It also requires a frank awareness that the other person is not perfect, just like we're not (we just don't see it all the time, since we're on the inside looking out). Yes, the rush will slow, the heat will fade, the mystery will soon unravel. In order to survive the dreaded aging process, a couple must share intellectual, emotional, and spiritual capital beyond mere instant attraction. While physical chemistry may be the magnet that pulls us together, without all the deeper connections, the draw will eventually weaken and fall apart.

FOLLOW-UP

One year later DSI discovered that both parties are involved in serious monogamous relationships and seem very happy. Mr. Silverstein is dating a woman who practices Tantric yoga, with whom he has embarked on a sexual journey. And Ms. Kessler is married to a great guy who's particularly adept with his tongue.

DOES YOUR PARTNER SUFFER FROM SEXUAL SELFISHNESS?

If he exhibits four or more of the following symptoms, consider him *guilty* as charged:

1. A double-standard regarding sex acts, such as demanding that oral sex be performed, without equal reciprocation

2. A focus on one's own orgasm at the expense of a partner's broader level of satisfaction

3. Lack of eye contact and/or emotional content during sexual interaction, which can range from a rush to intercourse without "foreplay," to an apparent focus on the act of sex rather than the sexual partner

4. Reliance on the "performance" of acts drawn from pornographic movies without regard to the other person's pleasure or express preferences

5. A lack of communication about sex, an unwillingness to try new things, and/or an effort to block out, rather than respond to, a partner's level of arousal during interactions

6. A willfully ignorant assumption that a woman has achieved orgasm during intercourse, also known as the "don't ask, don't tell policy." This lethal combination—lying by omission/willful ignorance—is undoubtedly the most common reason why women's sexual needs often languish in bitter silence.

DSI MOST WANTED FUGITIVE

WANTED FOR:

INABILITY TO COMMUNICATE; FEAR OF LONG-TERM RELATIONSHIPS; PASSIVE-AGGRESSIVE BEHAVIOR; FAILURE TO COMMIT

Ivan Harrison

Aliases: Ivan the Error-ful; The In-Between Machine; Sour Fickle; Ivan the Not-So-Great

DESCRIPTION

Date of Birth: 1973

Place of Birth: Rochester, NY

Height: 5' 9"

Weight: Approximately 170

Build: Average

Hair: Gray

Eyes: Blue

Complexion: Olive

Sex: Male

Nationality: American

Occupation: Insurance salesman

Remarks: Mr. Harrison is a serial dead-ender who drives women away through failing to commit or even talk about the possibility of a future. He also suffers from a severe case of the "grass is greener" syndrome, leading him to devalue the women he's involved with for failing to live up to the ones he's yet to meet. Mr. Harrison is well known for his ability to avoid conversations involving his emotions and/or where a relationship is headed. This is achieved through a variety of techniques, including grunting noises in lieu of verbal responses and failure to make eye contact during "serious" conversations. Mr. Harrison tends to engage in long-term, dead-end relationships that start slow, move slower, and end abruptly.

Scars and Marks: Mr. Harrison has few distinguishing features, other than being prematurely gray, a condition he refuses to alter, which he holds responsible for the kinds of women he attracts and his failure to obtain a promotion that should have been offered without him having to ask.

CAUTION

IVAN HARRISON IS WANTED IN CONNECTION WITH A TEN-YEAR RELATIONSHIP-KILLING SPREE THAT SPANS SEVERAL COUNTIES IN UPSTATE NEW YORK. OFTEN DE-SCRIBED AS "AN AVERAGE SCHMO," MR. HARRISON'S MILD MANNER AND LETHAL LACK OF DISTINGUISHING FEATURES MAKE HIM PARTICULARLY HARD TO IDENTIFY.

THIS INDIVIDUAL IS KNOWN TO LULL WOMEN INTO BELIEVING HE IS A GOOD CATCH. HE IS ALSO CONSIDERED ARMED WITH AN ARSENAL OF EXCUSES, INCLUDING "IT'S NOT YOU, IT'S ME"; "I JUST DON'T THINK I'M READY FOR SOMETHING LIKE THIS"; AND "I'M COMING OFF OF A DIFFICULT RELATIONSHIP AND AM NOT LOOKING FOR ANY-THING SERIOUS RIGHT NOW."

IF YOU HAVE ANY INFORMATION CONCERNING THIS RELATIONSHIP FELON, PLEASE CONTACT YOUR LOCAL DSI OFFICE.

REWARD

At this point in time there are no officially sanctioned rewards out for Mr. Harrison. However, DSI has learned of several unsanctioned bounties being offered for Mr. Harrison's capture, funded mainly by women he has previously dated.

SIX:

ON THE CLOCK

THE CASE OF THE RELATIONSHIP
RUINED BY BAD TIMING

THE DSI 911

The following was a unique case in that it presented a situation in which the ARSE was not a person, but rather a circumstance—in this instance, bad timing. The DSI 911 call came in from both parties, their concern being whether their relationship could overcome a complex web of external impediments. The woman, Ms. Peterson, was just getting over a broken engagement, in which she had been the aggrieved party. While she had developed strong feelings for Mr. Lakind, she feared she lacked the emotional readiness to enter into another serious relationship at this time. Mr. Lakind's concerns were largely career-related. His job took him to various client sites both domestically and abroad for unpredictable lengths of time. This made it difficult for the parties to spend substantial quality time together or fall into a natural rhythm. Despite these extenuating factors, both felt the relationship was worthy of further investigation and called upon DSI experts to determine whether their relationship was doomed by bad timing.

PRELIMINARY DIAGNOSIS

Bad timing is not, in the classic sense, a "disorder." Rather, it is one of the countless environmental factors that impact a relationship from the "outside." Many couples speak of finding their partners "at precisely the right time" or feel they were "destined to meet at that particular moment," which is a romantic shorthand for saying they were ready, willing, and able to commit to a long-term relationship. Differences in goals, politics, religion, hobbies, and even aesthetics can prove disastrous at this highly sensitive stage of the game. Add to the mix external hurdles, and the couple may be in for a bumpy ride.

When DSI speaks of "bad timing," we are referring to the typical case of "the right person, wrong moment." But what does this actually mean? In some cases, bad timing is simply an excuse. Life is complex, after all, and the world does not stop moving so two people can date and fall in love. For busy professionals with hectic lives, "bad timing" is not the exception; it's the rule. Yet we are a hard-working lot of multitaskers, and what could be more compelling than finding someone with whom to share the rest of our hectic, crazy lives?

Nonetheless, there are cases, such as this one, where even the most rigorous massage may not be sufficient to work out the inevitable kinks and aches.

PARALLEL CASE ANECDOTALS

"My ex claimed we wanted different things, and that it was just a case of bad timing. But what I think she really meant was that I couldn't give her the thing she wanted, right now, in terms of being a provider. I tried to explain to her that I had a long-term plan for us, but she wasn't ready to listen."

—Steve, 33

"I'm not sure if Peter will ever be ready for a relationship. Certainly not while we were dating. He was perfect on paper, but I think he still had some oats to sow. Maybe I just met him at the wrong time. Who knows what would have happened had we dated five years from now?"

—Lola, 27

"Scott and I were hot and heavy for a year until he got accepted into law school. Then everything suddenly changed overnight. He said he needed to focus on his grades, but I knew if he'd really wanted to make it work with us, he could have. I think it was more a question of us moving in different directions in our lives. P.S. I recently heard through a friend of a friend that he got engaged to a woman in his first-year class."

—Beth, 24

CASE SPECIFICS

The Dupe: Jodi Peterson
Age: 31
Location: Chicago, IL
Occupation: Teacher
Hair: Brown
Eyes: Blue
Height: 5'9"
Weight: 146

RELATIONSHIP RAP SHEET/EX FILES

Past Serious Relationships: 7
Total Number of Sexual Partners: 11
Exes Still in Contact: 5

Interpersonal Infractions

November 1999

After reluctantly agreeing to go on a blind date with the son of one of her mother's colleagues, Ms. Peterson nonetheless found herself having a lovely time. Her date took her to a fine restaurant, and they appeared to have a lot in common, including a love of Tolstoy, a fondness for old Hitchcock films, and a preference for chocolate over vanilla-based ice creams. But when Ms. Peterson learned that her date was thinking of quitting his job as a high-level marketing executive to become a kindergarten teacher, she suddenly developed a migraine, which prevented her from completing the dessert course or ever going out with him again.

Mating Misdemeanors

December 2000

When Ms. Peterson's boyfriend of six months failed to use "the L word" after she cooked him a candlelit gourmet meal and gave him a blow job for dessert, she demanded to know where the relationship was heading. When he hedged, she showed him to the door, stating, "I'm not getting any younger." (She was 24 at the time.)

February 2002

Ms. Peterson broke up with a man she'd been dating for three weeks (i.e., a total of two dinners and one Sunday brunch) during the third of six courses at a five-star French restaurant on Valentine's Day for failing to bring her more than flowers, informing him, "Silver earrings are the bare minimum to convey readiness for emotional attachment."

Flirtatious Felonies

April 2004

Ms. Peterson took down the phone number of an attractive investment banker at a party thrown by a boyfriend of eight months, "just in case" things didn't work out. When she broke up with her boyfriend a few months later for failing to discuss cohabitation by the one-year point, she called the banker for a date, well aware he was a good friend of her distraught ex-boyfriend. The banker declined the date and hung up on her, calling her a "heartless shrew."

Psychographic Thumbnail

Raised in a professional double-income household in which her mother, a corporate marketing V.P., was the primary breadwinner and her father, a part-time caterer, was in charge of supervising all domestic matters, Ms. Peterson and her younger sister were strongly encouraged to achieve (though "pushed" is the word a child psychologist might use). While Ms. Peterson's sister became a surgeon and has yet to marry, Ms. Peterson decided she wanted to go the more traditional route. Although she intends to continue teaching after she has children, she would like to be more of a "presence" than her own mother, who was frequently away on travel. Nonetheless, both she and her sister were successfully trained from an early age not to put up with second-class treatment from men. While her younger sister has dated very little, focusing almost entirely on her career (much like her mother), Ms. Peterson always evidenced a strong emotional need to be part of a couple (more like her father).

Even as a teenager, she was the type who always "needed" a boyfriend. Her dating life shows a pattern of moving from one relationship to the next, with little downtime in between. However, she is also a self-confident, strong-minded woman, and she doesn't hesitate to break things off with a boyfriend when she feels she's been unjustly treated. A no-nonsense person, she doesn't generally give men a second chance. While some of her friends consider this inflexible, Ms. Peterson says she is simply standing up for herself. Her most recent relationship ended after she found out her fiancé had cheated on her several months earlier. They had been together for three years, and "cutting things off" was the toughest thing she'd ever had to do. But she felt certain she'd made the right decision and never looked back (at least consciously).

The Arse: Jason Lakind
Age: 33
Location: Chicago, IL
Occupation: Business strategy consultant
Hair: Brown
Eyes: Blue
Height: 5'11"
Weight: 165

RELATIONSHIP RAP SHEET/EX FILES

Past Serious Relationships: 3
Total Number of Sexual Partners: 14
Exes Still in Contact: 5

Interpersonal Infractions

March 2000

After a several month flirtation with a woman who worked at another branch of his company, Mr. Lakind canceled a date planned three weeks earlier to attend an optional meeting on life/work balance that he knew many of the senior-level officers would be attending, explaining, "Face-time is my number one priority at this juncture in my career." She thereupon refused to accept his "rain check."

October 2003

Mr. Lakind fell asleep during a presentation by the female head of Human Resources (whom he'd taken out for dinner the previous Friday) during a workshop on sexual harassment in the workplace.

Mating Misdemeanors

August 2000

At the age of twenty-eight, Mr. Lakind decided to go back and get his M.B.A. at night, failing to mention this fact to his thirty-one-year-old girlfriend, whom he'd been dating for two years. Announcing at break-fast on the last Monday in August that he had something important he wanted to discuss with her at dinner on Friday night, she was certain he was going to whisk her off for a romantic holiday weekend and pop the question. When she arrived at the restaurant in a new silk dress with her hair professionally styled, he poured her a glass of champagne and pro-posed as follows: "I'm afraid I'll no longer be available to see you more than one night per week, since I've enrolled in a two-year M.B.A. pro-gram at the University of Chicago, which meets three nights a week and requires a hefty workload." His girlfriend promptly burst into tears and ran out of the restaurant and, subsequently, his life.

Flirtatious Felonies

April 2004

Mr. Lakind asked a woman he'd gone out with a few times in business school to accompany him to an office cocktail party. When one of his single male bosses approached, saying, "Where on earth did you discover this beauty?" Mr. Lakind replied, "We're not that serious, if you want to go out with her." The woman thereupon slapped him in the face and later left on the arm of his boss, who exchanged a kindly wink with Mr. Lakind on the way out.

Psychographic Thumbnail

The product of a double-income family, Mr. Lakind grew up in a some-what traditional household, with his father holding a prestigious, de-manding job as a financial analyst, and his mother working strictly 9:00 to 5:00 as an academic administrator at a local college. He and his older sister were raised to conceive of a marriage as a partnership, but generally held the view that the woman was primarily in charge of parenting and the father was the principle wage-earner.

While Mr. Lakind has been a prolific dater, he has not had many se-rious or deep relationships. He considers this "an occupational hazard," explaining: "I work a lot of hours in a lot of different cities. That doesn't leave much time for little extras like love. I've had no time for real relationships," reported Mr. Lakind. "I'm too busy trying to earn a living." According to a DSI profiling system, Mr. Lakind exhibits a mild tendency to use work to avoid emotional intimacy and as an excuse from having to form close ties to the women he dates. In addition, his hyperbolic need to succeed in the workplace evidences certain self-esteem issues, including a belief that he does not "deserve" a long-term relationship unless he is "a good provider," much like his father was.

RELATIONSHIP RECONNAISSANCE

Ms. Peterson and Mr. Lakind met at an evening concert during one of Chicago's outdoor summer music festivals. Both lifelong jazz fans, their eyes fixed upon each other across a grassy field as the piano tinkled "Misty." They often reminisce how the evening had an almost mystical aura to it, like "something out there was pulling us together," said Mr. Peterson. Their first few dates revolved around this mutual interest, though they soon discovered they had more in common than just music. Both had been in serious relationships before. Both knew what it felt like when something was "there." And both agreed that this had the makings of something real, even after only a month of dating. As summer mellowed into fall, the two began spending a great deal of time together. Mr. Lakind often teased Ms. Peterson that, if she wasn't careful, she would single-handedly ruin his hopes of making partner.

Their first long weekend together involved apple picking and hiking in Northern Wisconsin, arranged by Ms. Peterson. It was here that Mr. Lakind suffered his first inkling that there might be lingering reverberations from Ms. Peterson's broken engagement, a relationship she'd severed a few months earlier upon finding a "curious file" marked "personal" on her fiancé's computer containing old correspondence detailing a sexual liaison with a coworker. While hiking through the woods with Mr. Lakind, Ms. Peterson became visibly upset and started crying. When Mr. Lakind asked what was troubling her, she screamed, "I was supposed to get married here a week from tomorrow!" and stormed off. While Mr. Lakind was disturbed that Ms. Peterson had taken him to the very place she'd planned to marry her ex-boyfriend, he chose to swallow his discomfort and be supportive. "I figured it was closure, and that she was taking back something precious that had been stolen. In a way, I was flattered." Afterward, Ms. Peterson apologized, stating, "I want you to know, I'm totally over that cheating asshole."

Things continued at a brisk pace, the couple marveling at how compatible they were and how lucky they'd met on that magical summer night, until Mr. Lakind received his long-awaited promotion. As a new junior partner in the company, Mr. Lakind was given far more responsibility (and money). But his management duties required him to travel more frequently. This meant he was no longer on the road one or two nights a week, but three or four. His schedule became unpredictable, and his mood sometimes irritable. He was tired, stressed, jet-lagged, and worried that he would fail at his new position and ruin his chances of becoming a good provider for Ms. Peterson. He did not convey these fears to Ms. Peterson, however, considering them unmanly. As a result, Ms. Peterson accused him of relegating her to secondary status. Mr. Lakind understood that Ms. Peterson was feeling neglected and apologized for his schedule, promising things would ease up once he had an opportunity to prove himself, at which point "they" wouldn't have to worry about "the future." While Ms. Peterson was happy Mr. Lakind envisioned such a future with her, she worried what he was doing all those nights on the road. Mr. Lakind was well aware of what Ms. Peterson suspected, since whenever he went away, she'd call his hotel room several times and make him say, "I am not a cheating asshole."

DATE SCENE RECONSTRUCTION

Three Months into Dating: Chicago Blues

LOCALE: Don't B Flat Jazz Land Café, downtown Chicago

Synopsis: When a favorite saxophonist reported he was coming out of retirement to give a one-night only concert on a Tuesday evening in October to commemorate the fiftieth anniversary of his career, Ms. Peterson asked

Mr. Lakind if he might be able to get off work early to attend. It still being two months away, Mr. Lakind happily agreed. When she reminded Mr. Lakind several times in the week preceding the concert, he mentioned that he might have to meet her there to finish up a little extra work for a project that was due the following Monday. Ms. Peterson was a good sport, thrilled to be going to the concert with Mr. Lakind. On the night in question, Ms. Peterson waited dutifully outside the hall from 7:30 P.M., when they were supposed to meet, until 8:30 P.M., the seating being first-come-first-serve only. Mr. Lakind did not pick up his cell phone, which was typical during a busy work stretch, and by the time he arrived at 9:00 P.M. the concert was sold out. The couple left in sullen silence, in separate cars.

Witness Testimony: A bouncer at the club commented, "That dame was the sweetest thing I've seen in years. I can't believe he left her standing out there in the cold. I'll tell you one thing, the way she iced him over, he sure ain't gonna be getting any honey anytime soon."

Five Months into Dating: Christmas Party Punch

LOCALE: Rolling Oaks Country Club of Chicago

Synopsis: For many of the employees at the consulting firm where Mr. Lakind worked, the annual Christmas Party was the highlight of their yearly social calendar. The CEO pulled out all the stops, allowing his underlings to get a taste of the highlife with an endless river of champagne and a menu fit to make the Duke of Windsor tip his hat in homage. For all the women who had the good fortune to attend, the purchase of a ball gown fit to grace the hallowed halls absorbed every titter of conversation in the ladies lavatory for months in advance. Ms. Peterson was anxious to make a good appearance, knowing proper presentation was critical to Mr. Lakind. She spent $840 on a pewter taffeta gown (not the norm on her meager teacher's salary), purchasing coordinating kitten heels for another $460 and had her hair, makeup, and nails done to boot. Mr. Lakind looked dashing when he picked her up wearing a full black tux and took her via black stretch limo to the gala event. Every pair of eyes remained glued on the couple as they sauntered elegantly down the stairs to the main ballroom. After introducing her to all his bosses, without bothering with those at or below his rank, they were invited to sit at the CEO's table—a significant coup for Mr. Lakind. Thereupon, he spent the entire evening immersed in a discussion of long-term corporate strategy with the doddering old geezer without once asking Ms. Peterson to dance or remarking how beautifully the moonlight shimmered in her eyes.

Witness Testimony: A waiter at the country club remarked, "I don't think I've ever seen a woman go from looking like Princess Di on her wedding day to a kid whose father just ran over the family dog. It was sad, man. That guy of hers should be shot without a last meal or nothing!"

Seven Months into Dating: Sweet and Sour Magnolia

LOCALE: The Magnolia Blossom Inn, Charleston, Virginia

Synopsis: After a long and brutal stretch at work, Mr. Lakind decided to make it up to Ms. Peterson by arranging a weekend at an old Southern inn that boasted beautiful gardens, charming antique furnishings, and romantic fireside dinners in the intimate parlor. When they arrived, however, Ms. Peterson was dismayed to discover a red Chevy pickup parked in the driveway outside and a pot-bellied pig strolling around the side yard, which the pimpled son of the owners introduced as, "Bacon Bits." Deeming their room "shabby" rather than rustic, the clawfoot tub "rundown" rather than charming, and the homemade biscuits and marmalade "a far cry from high tea at the Ritz," Ms. Peterson insisted they leave at once, without reveling in the burnished glow of sunset over the lily pond past the honeysuckle-perfumed gazebo, where Mr. Lakind had planned to whisper "I love you" to Ms. Peterson for the very first time.

Witness Testimony: Said Billy Bob, Jr., heir to the Magnolia Blossom legacy: "That poor guy was worse off than Bacon Bits is gonna be after

Easter dinner. I could tell he was real hard up on that sourpuss, too. Dang shame it is too, all that romantic nonsense going to waste and all."

FORENSIC ASSESSMENT AND EVIDENTIARY ANALYSIS

Physical Evidence

The physical evidence gathered from both parties was consistent with a finding of "bad timing."

In Ms. Peterson's case, certain items in her dwelling indicated she was not "totally over that cheating loser," to wit:

- Prominently displayed photos and keepsakes from her last relationship, including emails, a framed wedding invitation, and daily printouts of Google searches on her ex-fiancé's new girlfriend, a petite food columnist for a popular bridal magazine, whom she found out about through a mutual friend after needling her for months about how she was "totally over that cheating asshole, and just curious."

- She still maintained some contact with his parents and other family members.

- When Mr. Lakind asked if he could use one of the now-empty drawers in her dresser previously occupied by her ex-fiancé, she said, "that place is reserved."

On Mr. Lakind's side of the equation, DSI found the following:

- In response to a recent "work-life balance initiative" undertaken by his company, Mr. Lakind stated on his Travel Restrictions Request: "Available as needed without limitation."

- Pursuant to emails received from personnel stating, "Consistent with the company's new work-life balance initiative, all client meetings can be attended in person or via video teleconferencing," Mr. Lakind had replied: "N.A."

→ Memos confirming that Mr. Lakind had "voluntarily opted out of taking unused vacation and personal days for the year without compensation."

→ On the interoffice whiteboard reserved for recreational purposes, under "name of spouse or domestic partner," next to Mr. Lakind's name, someone had scribbled in "Mrs. Promotion."

Forensic Metrics

Co-Dependency Assessment Correlation (CoDAC)

While Ms. Peterson's dating record indicates a history of always having a partner, the CoDAC indicated that while there is some evidence of dependency in her past, she is emotionally capable of being alone and does not suffer from true codependency. Her reading was low enough to suggest such minor dependency could be overcome through advanced level of self-awareness and therapeutic treatment.

Degree of Occupational Limitation Test (DOLT)

The DOLT analysis is used to determine how much a party to a relationship is relying on career to protect him or her from emotional relationships. Mr. Lakind demonstrates a moderate tendency to avoid intimacy through work compounded by an inclination to correlate his value as a partner by his level of professional success. It is typical for men and women to "hide" behind their work when relationships get too serious. In the case at hand, there is also the added layer of having Mr. Lakind's self-esteem wrapped up in his working life, which makes the DOLT reading critical. Mr. Lakind's DOLT reading indicated that he was indeed limiting himself and his emotional range and that he was using the workplace as an excuse.

DSI FINDING

This case presented an interesting set of facts. While our original mandate was to gauge the impact of external timing factors on overall relationship viability, doing so required a preliminary assessment of the psychological readiness of the individual parties for emotional intimacy. Our findings yield empirical proof of "bad timing" factors, but they do not rise to the level of an "incurable defect." The parties appear ready, willing, and able to devote significant time and effort to improving self- and mutual-awareness, leading to a reasonable likelihood of long-term relationship success.

RELATIONSHIP REHAB

Consistent with the above determination, DSI has outlined a number of critical short- and long-term goals for each of the parties to facilitate greater intimacy and emotional satisfaction, as follows:

- Mr. Lakind must engage in a course of individual therapy to help him dissociate self-esteem from professional achievement.

- Ms. Peterson must engage in a course of individual therapy to resolve lingering feelings of anger, betrayal, and resentment from her last relationship and make a deliberate effort to avoid globalizing her negative experience into an overarching distrust of men in general and Mr. Lakind in particular.

- Mr. Lakind must make a concerted effort to achieve a better work-life balance and take keener advantage of opportunities to work remotely rather than on-site to increase domestic quality time.

- Ms. Peterson must make an effort to understand and appreciate Mr. Lakind's ambitious nature and concomitant desire to be a good provider, consistent with both their long-term goals, and become more comfortable engaging in solo activities.

DATING DIAGNOSTIC

In today's interconnected, high-speed world, we're all victims of bad timing. Every day we make choices that prioritize work obligations over personal relationships. We sacrifice a romantic lunch to spend more time slaving away on a project that may benefit us slightly if we do a thousand more just like it. We delay instant gratification to keep our eyes fastened on the "big picture." Rather than revel in the beauty of the moment, as the romantic poets would put it, we pencil in our pleasure for a more convenient time.

In short: we aspire more than we desire. As a result, our fantasies are often painted in the color of material objects instead of sunsets, and we tremble for the taste of champagne more than we do for summer rain. So, fine, that's the world we live in and who we are. While you may protest this as cynical or profess to soften at the lilt of "love can conquer all," the reality is our relationships often get short shrift. They get negotiated rather than experienced. Our romantic partners, no matter how lovely, come marked with a price tag of effort and time, rare commodities we are not so easy to part with unless we see a payoff down the line.

Just like bad timing and work pressure, being on the rebound is more the rule than the exception. Regardless of how it's touted as a romantic "no-no," we are sexually active adults, and seldom do we find ourselves perfectly free from past relationships. And, you know what? That's fine, too.

So what it all comes down to is a simple balancing act. Yes, there are scheduling conflicts. Of course there are temperamental differences. And forever there will be unfinished emotional puzzles languishing on our bottom shelves. But after the thrill of new love calms, the inescapable bottom line is: Do we still like each other? Do we enjoy each other's company? Do we see enough of the same big picture to blend those pictures into one broader landscape? And is it worth sacrificing some fraction of that most cherished commodity of time for the chance of waking up beside that other person decades down the line? If the thought inspires hope, rather than dread, in DSI's estimation, the answer is decidedly yes.

FOLLOW-UP

When DSI followed up with Mr. Lakind and Ms. Peterson a year later, it was no surprise to find the two of them living at the same address. Ms. Peterson still complained that Mr. Lakind worked too many hours, though not because she worried he would cheat on her, but because she liked feeling his heartbeat pressed against her when they listened to Miles Davis. Mr. Lakind was no longer obsessed with bringing in the most revenue at his job, because he already felt like a million dollars for having a woman like Ms. Peterson by his side. While they may have devoted a lot of time to planning the big picture, the fact of the matter remains, that picture was of them.

IS YOUR FOCUS ON FUTURE GOALS INTERFERING WITH YOUR ABILITY TO APPRECIATE, ENJOY, AND WORK ON A RELATIONSHIP TODAY?

If you answer yes to four or more of the following, it's time to rethink your priorities:

1. Do you have age-specific, rather than person- or job-specific, goals regarding any of the following: when you plan to be married; when you plan to have your first child; when you plan to have your second child; when you will buy your first apartment or house; when you will earn a six-figure salary?

2. Do you check your voicemail from work between the hours of midnight and 6:00 A.M. at least three times a week?

3. Have you rehearsed in your head what you will write to your alumni magazine upon accomplishing a certain prefabricated goal held for two

years or longer? Examples could include getting married and/or having a baby; finishing up an advanced degree; publishing a novel; producing a film; or getting a prestigious job.

4. If called upon to do a special project that could expedite a possible promotion, but could be passed on without penalty, would you cancel a romantic weeklong vacation scheduled more than three months in advance? Would you postpone your own honeymoon? (If so, no need to read further, you're prima facie guilty.)

5. Do you have a shelf/drawer/closet of snacks and meal substitutes sufficient to feed a family of four for a week?

6. When you answer your phone at home, do you mistakenly identify yourself by department or full name, followed by, "What do you want now?"

7. Do you keep two or more of the following at your office?

> A full set of clothes, including underwear and accessories

> A razor and shaving cream, Nair, or a home waxing kit

> Condoms or other forms of birth control

> A full set of condiments, bowls, plates, and silverware

> Remedies for headaches, stomach ailments, and insomnia

THE CASE OF THE MAN TOO CHEAP TO DATE

When the 911 call first came in, we thought it had to be a prank. A woman's voice, undulating with fury, ranted, "I can't take it anymore! Do you hear me? My boyfriend just gave me a salad for my fortieth birthday, which he plucked right out of his stinking garden. I'd like to pluck his sorry ass into the ground!"

Our dispatcher tried to calm the woman, concerned that she might be suffering from acute trauma. "Are you in any immediate danger?" we asked.

"What, are you crazy or something? How could I be in danger from a salad?" the woman sighed, sniffling.

"And what seems to be the problem with the salad? Is there too much water in the bottom? Is the lettuce wilted?" we inquired in a soothing voice.

"It's my fortieth birthday, and that tightwad gave me a leftover salad he'd prepared for our last big night out," she simmered. "Not even a friggin' crouton, that penny-pinching weasel."

At last we understood. The ARSE in question, one Mr. Alvin Rutter, was a cheapskate. A growing complaint among professional women, Mr. Rutter was of the fair ilk of "evolved men" who did not suffer any masculine jitters by "letting a woman treat." Priding himself on being the kind of guy who judged a woman by what she had on the inside [of her wallet], Mr. Rutter met the majority of his dates, like our complainant, Ms. Joy Bismark, through a free online dating service. Old and young; thin and fat; deaf, dumb, and blind, the only thing these lucky ladies had in common, other than dating Mr. Rutter of course, was a personal income above $100,000 per year.

As an emancipated man who celebrated the liberal mantra of equal work for equal pay, Mr. Rutter reveled in their successes. "Bravo," he'd applaud at their feminist pluck, by which point most of them, now stuck with a colossal bill, would say something to the effect of, "I'd like to pluck your sorry ass with a garden hoe."

Like many others before, Ms. Bismark had originally found Mr. Rutter's whimsical fondness for staring at clouds and naming them things like "Fluffy" and "Pudding Pup" charming. On the first two dates, he welcomed Ms. Bismark into his rustic (aka run-down) cottage (aka shack). There he wooed her with radicchio nurtured by his own loving, semiemployed hands, and doused her in the oil of his glowing affections. Ms. Bismark was enchanted with Mr. Rutter's love of nature and boyish pleasure in taking strolls by the public beach. It was during the third such date that Ms. Bismark felt it "only right" to reciprocate. "I'd consider it an honor," cheered Mr. Rutter, struck by a sudden yen for French cuisine, and selecting a romantic bistro with flickering candlelight by which to gaze at Ms. Bismark's plucky feminist eyes.

"A meal is always meant to be savored," he advised, taking the liberty of ordering the finest selection of appetizers, entrees, side dishes, salads, cheeses, more entrees, Pinot Noir, a seasonal fruit plate and dessert. Upon retrieving his doggy bag, Mr. Rutter opined: "The food here is extraordinary." Judging by grimacing waiters, Ms. Bismark suspected that this statement had been stated here before.

Ms. Bismark was a bit put off when the $375 bill was foisted on her. Sensing her disquiet, Mr. Rutter sensitively exclaimed, "I thank you for your splendid company," rather than the more prosaic, "but please, this is my treat, or do allow me to chip in." Still, she figured he would make up for it the next go around, and believed his comfort evidenced a "deep and growing attachment." Ms. Bismark was right on that count. Mr. Rutter did find himself becoming quite enamored with Ms. Bismark, especially when she laid down her platinum charge card, which induced the words: "I think I'm falling in love with you."

As rich in his ardor as he was poor at tendering tender, Ms. Bismark at last saw the fuel-saving re-chargeable light bulb. "You gave me a leftover salad for my fortieth birthday? You cheap bastard; we're through!"

"Oh," Mr. Rutter saddened. "Then do you mind terribly if I save this salad for another day?"

Ms. Bismark exercised her powers of DSI citizen arrest, taking Mr. Rutter into custody for "spendthrift dating habits well in advance of any mutual acceptance thereof" and a long history of relationship cheapness.

SEVEN:
CORPORATE PERKS

THE DSI 911

DSI received a call from one Edward Hornsby, who, as you've likely deduced, is a man. While the majority of DSI calls come in from women, there are plenty of cases where men are duped, too. This is one of them. Mr. Hornsby was disconsolate because he and his girlfriend worked at the same small company, and he believed external pressures were severely affecting the relationship. Moreover, his girlfriend had recently been promoted, and Mr. Hornsby was now working for her. "How can I work for someone I'm dating?" he gasped. "Aside from ethical issues, it just feels awkward. And on top of everything else, I feel like she's taking professional advantage of me. Either the job or the relationship has to go!"

PRELIMINARY DIAGNOSIS

DSI has determined a clear-cut example of NICEASS (Naughty Inter-Cubicle Exchanges Affair Syndrome and Situation). This condition is particularly common among coworkers in their mid-twenties to early thirties and ranges from engaging in salacious instant messaging to full-out affairs. Distinguishing this particular case from the typical lot of workplace romance disorders is the fact that it involves a role reversal with a male Weak Willie (WW) and a female Boss on Wheels (BOW), whose work dynamic and office personalities were reflected in their romantic interactions.

PARALLEL CASE ANECDOTALS

"I never thought I'd date a man I worked with but, lo and behold, Tom and I started seeing each other after a corporate offsite. We both admitted that we had feelings for one another, and it just kind of blossomed. Fortunately, we work in different departments. Sure, we spend a lot of time talking about our company, but I can go weeks without seeing him at the office."

—Connie, 28

"I'm sure choosing a coworker for an affair was not the wisest choice I could have made, but there was something about the fact that we had this shared part of our lives that made it compelling. And, we were already spending so much time together that it seemed natural."

—Paul, 38

"The old saying goes you shouldn't eat where you sleep, and, unfortunately, it holds true, especially when you are trying to end something. The fact that Monica and I had to see each other every single day at work made us stay together much longer than we should have. It also made it very uncomfortable once it ended. I had to ask for a transfer, things got so out of control."

—Mark, 29

CASE SPECIFICS

The Dupe: Edward Hornsby
Age: 28
Location: San Francisco, CA
Occupation: Copywriter, Golden Gate Creative Partners
Hair: Brown
Eyes: Brown
Height: 6'
Weight: 165

RELATIONSHIP RAP SHEET/EX FILES

Past Serious Relationships: 3
Total Number of Sexual Partners: 5
Exes Still in Contact: 3

Interpersonal Infractions

➤ History of being passive

➤ Often sacrifices his own feelings to keep failing relationships going

➤ Prefers older women who have something to teach him

Mating Misdemeanors

November 2000

Takes a copywriting course at a local arts institute and develops a crush on the instructor, an attractive Ph.D. student five years his senior. At the final class, he works up the nerve to tell her how much he enjoyed her veiled references to Roland Barthes. As he prepares to walk out the door, she asks him out for a "cappuccino" (drawing quotation marks in the air) and they begin dating. They spend four wonderful months together, enjoying the same French art films, Russian literature, and paddle tennis. Then she invites him to meet her parents over vegan Thanksgiving at their ocean-view estate in Tiburon, California. Her parents, trust fund kids with Marxist leanings, take an instant liking to Mr. Hornsby, particularly impressed that his mother put herself through college at the age of forty and went on to become a celebrated figure in left-wing politics. The four of them take long walks, sip wine naked in the family hot tub, and, of course, discuss Hannah Arendt. But when the weekend ends, Mr. Hornsby grows sullen, telling his girlfriend he's not good enough for her. After two heart-wrenching months trying to persuade him otherwise, she reluctantly breaks things off with him.

August 2002

Meets a sales executive, twelve years older than him, in the laundry room of his building. She immediately tells him that she finds him attractive and would like to "get to know him better." Although he's not sure how he feels about her, since he tends to be slow in developing romantic interests, he figures he might as well give it a shot. They date for five months and, owing largely to convenience, are soon spending every night together. Realizing he is not, in fact, in love with her, he struggles for the courage to end the relationship, but is afraid to disappoint her. He lapses into depression and mopes around all the time, telling her he's too "bummed about the universe" to have sex. She tries to convince him to go on Prozac, but he refuses, saying "What's the point? The world will still suck. I'll just be too sedated to care." She finally breaks up with him, at which point his mood takes a sudden upswing.

Flirtatious Felonies

March 1999

Gets involved with a legally separated forty-five-year-old real estate broker, at the latter's insistence, after she helped find him a coveted no-fee apartment. Soon after they start dating, he agrees, against his better judgment, to help her track down secret financial records that her quasi-ex-husband kept in his office to prove his involvement in an "all-cash phar-maceutical business" (which she'd like to cash in on). Mr. Hornsby dons a pair of greasy overalls, provided by his girlfriend, and pretends to be a plumber. The husband, who has seen this routine before, punches him in the nose. When Mr. Hornsby begs off trying again as an electrician, the woman breaks up with him (to his immense relief).

Psychographic Thumbnail

Mr. Hornsby is a bit of mama's boy, having turned down a full scholar-ship to Yale to enroll at UC Berkeley part-time and help run his mother's gubernatorial campaigns. This is where he discovered his love and talent for creative marketing. His sensitive nature makes him an excellent copy-writer, as he is able to hone in on consumer weaknesses and desires. His intelligent, soft-spoken manner and wry wit make him extremely attrac-tive to assertive women. He, in turn, is particularly drawn to women who are comfortable taking the lead.

The relationships usually start off well, with his girlfriends praising him for being "unlike any man [they] have ever dated before, in a good way." There is no game-playing or failure to communicate. He is an ea-ger, attentive listener, honestly delighted to spend an entire evening dis-secting a single slight by an annoying friend. In bed, he is giving and sensitive, deeply concerned with his lovers' pleasure and oblivious to a lit-tle razor stubble or a few extra pounds.

All of this makes it that much harder when he suddenly decides that the woman he is dating, whom he respects and loves so dearly, is too good for him. While at first they are flattered, unaccustomed to such hu-mility in a man, eventually it becomes frustrating and flat-out annoying. The fact that he has caused his lovers distress further convinces him of his unworthiness and the dynamic eventually spirals politely down the drain.

In DSI terminology, Mr. Hornsby is a classic Weak Willie (WW), an emotionally frail man who lacks the backbone to survive in the real world.

The Arse: Martha Singer
Age: 33
Location: San Francisco, CA
Occupation: Vice president, Golden Gate Creative Partners
Hair: Red
Eyes: Blue
Height: 5'3"
Weight: 120

RELATIONSHIP RAP SHEET/EX FILES

Past Serious Relationships: 4
Total Number of Sexual Partners: 9
Exes Still in Contact: 1

Interpersonal Infractions

➤ Majority of relationships have been contentious and all but one (Mr. Hornsby) ended badly

➤ Generally has been the one to "wear the pants" in a relationship

➤ Is competitive in all aspects of her life, including love affairs and sexual situations

➤ Tends to like having a man in her life and grows insecure when she is alone for too long

Mating Misdemeanors

August 1993
After her college roommate confided a traumatic incident as a toddler wherein she mistook a jar of mayonnaise for her "ba-ba," resulting in an aversion to milky fluids, Ms. Singer informs her roommate's boyfriend

that she will do all the things her roommate won't. The boyfriend takes the bait, and the two begin dating. When her roommate takes an unexplained leave of absence, the boyfriend moves into her dorm room. Ms. Singer suddenly finds herself bored with him and decides to amuse herself by sleeping with two of his friends.

May 1997

After getting a B+ in one of her business strategy classes at UCLA, Ms. Singer goes to speak with her professor, asking if she can earn extra credit to pull herself into the A range. The professor, a nice-looking thirty-two-year-old with a wedding ring on his left hand and photographs of a chubby woman nursing a baby on his desk, tells her that "the grade is, unfortunately, final." Ms. Singer pouts and pulls her hands over her face, crying: "My parents will kill me if I get anything under an A! My father was an army lieutenant general!" [Ms. Singer's father taught guitar.] She then falls into his arms in a fit of tears. Several months later, during the final stages of his divorce proceeding, Ms. Singer finesses her 4.0 GPA into a swanky job at a major advertising firm with offices in LA and San Francisco. She chooses the San Francisco location, causing her to "temporarily" move out of the professor's apartment.

January 1999

During a company-wide team-building event in Aspen, Ms. Singer tips the concierge to give her the room adjoining the CEO's, who happens to be traveling with his wife and five-year-old twin boys. Although back in Ms. Singer's home there hangs a parka covered in lift tickets from double diamond trails, she finds herself in need of assistance on the bunny slope, where the CEO is tending to his wife and children. He's eager to instruct the young woman in all things pertaining to the use of a pole, and Ms. Singer clumsily trips right onto him, causing the two to tumble over each other into a snowy drift. When the CEO asks if she is okay, she whimpers, "I think I sprained my upper thighs. I should probably go and check it." Telling his wife he fears a lawsuit, he escorts Ms. Singer back to her hotel room and checks in on her both nights after his wife and children are asleep. When they return from the ski trip, Ms. Singer gets promoted to a position directly under him.

Flirtatious Felonies

February–May 2002

While Ms. Singer was engaged in a long-distance relationship, she developed an attraction for a young messenger at her new job. One early Friday evening, a few hours before her boyfriend was due to arrive, she had an epiphany of sorts and called the service, requesting an emergency run to her apartment. "This box must get off immediately. Please send Carlos at once," she demanded. "Carlos is finishing up his last run for the day, but I can send over our evening girl," said the receptionist. "I must have Carlos at once," exclaimed Ms. Singer, incensed. "He's already finishing up his shift," was the reply. "Did you just call me a shit?" asked Ms. Singer. "What are you crazy? I said 'shift,' not 'shit'!" responded the receptionist. "Well, I have it on tape that you said I was a crazy shit." The receptionist sighed. "Carlos will be right over to service you, ma'am." And he was. And he did, several times, in fact. Right until Ms. Singer's boyfriend walked in the door, whereupon she signed the receipt for successful delivery of her box.

Psychographic Thumbnail

Ms. Singer is a spitfire who never takes no for an answer. The youngest of five and the only girl, her parents were intent on "trying for a girl' no matter how long it took, a decision which required Mr. Singer to give guitar lessons on weekends and Mrs. Singer to babysit three afternoons a week for extra cash.

From an early age, Ms. Singer rankled at the squalor of her home in Northeast Philly. "That one's a princess," her father would beam proudly at her snobbery. "She was worth all the sacrifice," echoed her mother. With four older brothers, Ms. Singer was a tomboy when nobody was watching and a princess when necessity required it. She would bite, scratch, and kick her older brothers with a demon force they could not match with might. And then she'd cry as daintily as a "little angel" (which happened to be her father's pet name for her) whenever one of "those nasty boys" dared to raise a pinkie. More comfortable with boys than girls, she knew just how to win her way in any situation. Once puberty enhanced her arsenal, she was undefeatable. While Ms. Singer preferred to have a few popular female best friends for appearance's sake, she was not the type of girl to go blabbering on the phone about why "so-and-so doesn't notice me." Because so-and-so did notice her—and she noticed.

Ms. Singer managed to get a straight A average in college, with the help a few male friends along the way, after which she chose a job in a large advertising agency, at the suggestion of a certain professor. Several years and only two promotions later, she left to go to a boutique firm, hoping to move up more quickly. She has achieved a certain level of success in her career, even though she sometimes brushes up against coworkers in an aggressive manner.

In her romantic life, she exudes a similar energy and finds it very difficult, not to mention flat-out unnecessary, to compromise. She is quick to criticize, except with regard to herself, still feeling (and acting) like a princess. Like many modern women, she views career advancement as her top priority. Her disdain of the "squalor" she grew up with tips the balance toward workaholism. Yet despite this go-go attitude, she wants to find "the perfect husband," and have "two beautiful children, one boy and one girl." And, unlike her mother, she doesn't intend to get it wrong so many times in between. A person who is never happier than when she is busy, when she does find herself with a few hours to spare, the floodgates of her sexual and emotional needs come crashing down over everything in its path, often clouding her judgment. Ms. Singer does not like to be alone, which means Ms. Singer rarely is.

RELATIONSHIP RECONNAISSANCE

Mr. Hornsby and Ms. Singer met at their place of employment, Golden Gate Creative Partners, a boutique advertising agency known for cutting-edge creative work. Mr. Hornsby has worked at the agency since he graduated from college, while Ms. Singer has only been at the company for two years. The agency has fifty employees, and Mr. Hornsby and Ms. Singer had not worked on any of the same accounts when they first met. Nonetheless, as a small company with a "work-hard-play-hard" gestalt, they had frequent contact during eleven-hour workdays and social events. They began dating after a slow flirtation, ignited by Ms. Singer during one of the company's "pub nights." While Mr. Hornsby was wary of dating a coworker, Ms. Singer was aggressive, and Mr. Hornsby was unable to resist, owing to a strong attraction along with his compliant nature.

They were able to keep their relationship a secret for the first three months, and the illicit feeling gave it a strong sense of excitement. Both enjoyed the inside references and long sultry glances across the bullpen of cubicles where they worked. Long lunches would become groping sessions and the occasional business trip a Bacchanalian fest. Their out-of-work interactions were also quite enjoyable, as Ms. Singer preferred the convenience of having a man around during nonbusy periods. She genuinely liked Mr. Hornsby's understated manner, intellectual bent, and doting ways. For his part, Mr. Hornsby was smitten. He loved Ms. Singer's strength, drive, and voracious desire to be served, both in and out of bed. As a result, they were each committed to the idea of making the relationship work, even if it meant "coming out" to their employers. Ms. Singer further believed that management would make an exception for such a stellar woman and Mr. Hornsby. So rather than risk the embarrassment of being "found out," they formally announced themselves a couple one pub night. Their revelation was met with a toast of German lager, although a senior partner warned them not to "bring their quarrels to the office."

Though Mr. Hornsby's tenure at Golden Gate Creative Partners predated Ms. Singer's, his ascension was not as rapid. This he attributed to a native preference for remaining in the creative trenches over climbing the corporate ladder. Ms. Singer had no such qualms, and while she was brought in at the same title as Mr. Hornsby, she quickly rose to the level of vice president. At the six-month point of their relationship, she took over accounts to which Mr. Hornsby was assigned. She became, in effect, his day-to-day manager, causing a fair amount of teasing by the close-knit staff. While Ms. Singer made a concerted effort not to let the relationship impact her treatment of Mr. Hornsby, other coworkers began to complain of favoritism. These allegations fell on deaf ears to upper management, however, who knew Mr. Hornsby was "the best damn copywriter in the shop."

As a result of this success, Ms. Singer and Mr. Hornsby were able to stave off negative opinion from management and weather the situation for several months, until the problem became not their status as coworkers, but rather Ms. Singer. After Ms. Singer was promoted, Mr. Hornsby became convinced she was too good for him. Rather than attempt to disabuse Mr. Hornsby of this sense of inferiority, she exploited it by being more punitive and demanding than ever. By so doing, Ms. Singer inadvertently "saved" their relationship, because rather than becoming sullen, guilty, and distant as he had in previous relationships, Mr. Hornsby rose to the position of "servant." Nonetheless, their "odd" sadomasochistic tendencies have met with poor reviews in the workplace, Mr. Hornsby being dubbed a Weak Willie and Ms. Singer a Boss on Wheels.

They both agree that one of them must leave the company if their relationship is to continue, but neither of them is inclined to make the jump. Mr. Hornsby reached out to DSI to help resolve the situation.

DATE SCENE RECONSTRUCTION

One Month into Dating: Diaper Rash

LOCALE: Main Conference Room, Golden Gate Creative Partners

Synopsis: During a meeting with prospective clients, also attended by two senior partners, Ms. Singer pitched several ideas she'd gleaned from Mr. Hornsby in the course of her favorite bathtub game, "Pitch the Account," wherein she provided a "hypothetical" product and Mr. Hornsby supplied any number of original branding concepts. The agency won the account, and Ms. Singer was accorded credit for her "brilliant pitch." Mr. Hornsby thought it strangely coincidental that their game had been so closely related to an actual product, especially given the rather obscure nature—self-cleaning diaper bags—but chalked it up to kismet.

Witness Testimony: Coworkers in the meeting were later heard saying, "There is no way that bitch came up with that idea. That has Hornsby written all over it. She would sooner kick a baby in the ass than protect it from contaminated diapers." The client lead opined: "That sexy redhead has some good ideas," and subsequently requested that she lead the campaign.

Five Months into Dating: Bye Dinner at Andre

LOCALE: Chez Andre Restaurant

Synopsis: During what was supposed to be a romantic supper at a five-star restaurant "to discuss ideas" for their first weekend getaway, Ms. Singer instead asked Mr. Hornsby to "take a quick peek" at an account proposal, and then spent most of the meal on her cell phone with her boss (also Mr. Hornsby's boss), parlaying Mr. Hornsby's ideas into a lead position on an account. When Mr. Hornsby later questioned her about why she'd taken credit, she explained that once she used her slightly higher rank in the organization to land the account, she would, of course, give him "full credit" for his "creative input" and they could work together as a team. Mr. Hornsby grew quiet, but was unable to confront her about her dishonest behavior, sensing something about it "wasn't quite right." Ms. Singer deftly changed the subject to the "fabulous three-day weekend" she had planned for them at a deluxe spa in the Napa Valley, complete with nightly wine tastings, and he soon forgot what had been troubling him.

Witness Testimony: A busboy at the restaurant overheard the entire exchange between Mr. Hornsby and Ms. Singer; Ms. Singer and her cell phone; and Ms. Singer and her weekend pitch and declared, "She like totally played his ass. What a wanker."

Six Months into Dating: Step into My Parlor

LOCALE: Ms. Singer's Office

Synopsis: Soon after she was promoted, Ms. Singer called a team meeting at her new office to discuss how copywriters could work more efficiently, singling out Mr. Hornsby's work habits as an example of how "a talented worker could prove a detriment to overall productivity." While Ms. Singer claimed she was using him as an example, because his work was so valued that nobody minded that he neglected to pick up phone messages and emails (from *her*) when he was on a project, Mr. Hornsby thought she made him look stupid in front of his coworkers. Ms. Singer then explained that she had done it to create a smokescreen for their relationship, to prove that he wasn't being given special treatment.

Witness Testimony: Coworkers who attended the meeting were "stunned" that Ms. Singer would "torch Hornsby's Weak Willie so badly."

FORENSIC ASSESSMENT AND EVIDENTIARY ANALYSIS

Exhibit One

Upon preliminary investigation, DSI decrypted a "confidential journal" on Ms. Singer's hard drive that predated the couple's involvement. In it, she laid out her personal mission to "engage Mr. Hornsby's loyalty by all means necessary and harness his unrivaled talents to facilitate my promotion to upper management, and then fire him." A more recent journal entry noted an addendum to the original plan: "Mr. Hornsby represents an ideal husband prospect. Make recommendation to upper management to award him a significant severance package sufficient to cover large down payment; demote him to stay-at-home husband/father and private creative adviser."

Physical Evidence

An examination of certain physical evidence revealed the following signs of interoffice subterfuge and possible infidelity:

→ Network-fingerprinting revealed Ms. Singer had hacked into Mr. Hornsby's personal creative files under a bogus password she'd secured from an obliging member of the IT team, and then checked his "performance reviews" with a little help from a member of the custodial staff, prior to their involvement.

→ A confidential performance review by Ms. Singer of Mr. Hornsby's work assigned him an average "grade" with a recommendation for a generous severance package.

→ The return of a red thong from a member of the custodial staff, that Mr. Hornsby did not recognize, suggested a questionable interlude.

→ The twenty-five-year-old Help Desk supervisor appeared overly willing to respond to Ms. Singer's frequent requests for "special access," most occurring on late nights when the two were alone. This ran counter to their standard response: "Due to a system conversion, we cannot address individual technical issues at this time."

Forensic Metrics

Sexual Potency And Romantic Kinship (SPARK) Test

Utilizing the SPARK test, which determines baseline sexual chemistry and emotional compatibility of couples, DSI found the relationship between Mr. Hornsby and Ms. Singer failed to meet the core viability threshold, due to Ms. Singer's "advanced to severe" lack of emotional readiness for intimacy. Mr. Hornsby, though showing a sincere attachment to Ms. Singer, exhibited "moderate to advanced" issues of negative codependent self-worth, causing him to suffer feelings of inferiority and to "sacrifice his own needs." While the two had an active sex life, it lacked emotional passion. An Orgasm Veracity Assessment (OVA) further concluded that Ms. Singer had faked orgasms on multiple occasions in an effort to abridge sexual interactions and play "Pitch the Account" and other erotic work-based role-playing games.

Cellular Analysis Tapping Scan (CAT Scan)

A tap placed on Ms. Singer's electronic devices, including her cell phone and Blackberry, indicated that she was utilizing information and ideas given to her by Mr. Hornsby to advance her own career and to sabotage his once she'd vouchsafed her promotion. Intercepted emails proved Ms. Singer had initiated several discussions with upper management with regard to offering Mr. Hornsby a generous severance package and keeping him on as a freelance, off-site copywriter, as needed. She had further made efforts to have Mr. Hornsby's closest (and only remaining) friend at work transferred to the Los Angeles office in an effort to reduce his workplace satisfaction and induce him to take the package. Further linguistic analysis indicated that, while Ms. Singer had excellent management skills, her intellectual capacity was far below Mr. Hornsby's.

Watercooler Mole

DSI placed a field operative into Golden Gate Creative Partners. Our mole infiltrated Ms. Singer's group and was able to provide unbiased and real-time observations from coworkers. Generally speaking, the mole's findings were consistent with the initial diagnosis of NICEASS. Moreover, the mole indicated that "public opinion" sided heavily with Mr. Hornsby. Most coworkers felt Ms. Singer's motives were less than honorable, and they recognized that all of her newfound creative brilliance was coming from Hornsby. But mostly they wondered how any "self-respecting man," could take "all that pussy-whipping."

DSI FINDING

The physical evidence and forensic analysis in this case shows a particularly pernicious mutation of NICEASS, marked by nonromantic motives, sadism, and dissemblance on the part of Ms. Singer; and pathologic denial, ego-effacement, and masochism on Mr. Hornsby's end. Mr. Hornsby's initial call to DSI indicates his level of delusion. As a secondary finding, DSI has determined that Ms. Singer entered into the relationship for reasons that had more to do with career advancement than attraction to Mr. Hornsby. It should be noted, however, that to the extent Ms. Singer is capable of experiencing genuine emotions, she did experience them with/for Mr. Hornsby. Her calculated selection of him as a lover and suitable husband prospect reflects this fact. Mr. Hornsby was therefore not *altogether* deluded in believing that she wanted to work things out with him. Ms. Singer would, nonetheless, require intensive therapy to develop the capacity and self-awareness necessary to tap into whatever feelings she has and does not appear inclined to make such a commitment.

RELATIONSHIP REHAB

Contrary to the norm, this is a case in which, while both parties express a desire to stay in the relationship, DSI finds such an outcome inherently harmful to the psychic and emotional well-being of the parties. It is evident that Ms. Singer had ulterior motives in dating Mr. Hornsby. Despite the fact that she did develop an actual attachment along the way, her effective lack of emotional maturity and empathy preclude her from being able to engage in a meaningful relationship until she completes an intensive course of therapy. DSI therefore recommends the following:

→ Mr. Hornsby must take proactive steps to end his relationship with Ms. Singer at once.

→ From a purely pragmatic standpoint, Mr. Hornsby should come clean with upper management and prepare a written statement indicating how the relationship with Ms. Singer unjustifiably impacted his standing at work. He should also compile supporting evidentiary documents indicating that Ms. Singer stole his work product and called it her own.

➤ Mr. Hornsby must undertake a course of individual therapy to develop a stronger sense of boundaries and internalized ego, so he is less susceptible to environmental factors, and less inclined to measure his value as a romantic partner by the value he provides through self-sacrifice and service.

➤ Mr. Hornsby should undertake a temporary period of abstinence from romantic relationships as such emotional involvements tend to erode, rather than support, his fragile ego.

DATING DIAGNOSTIC

Despite the fact that many say they would never date a coworker, interoffice romances are extremely common. Intuitively, this makes sense. In comparison to our friends across the pond, "the typical American work[s] 350 more hours per year than the typical European," according to the Bureau of Labor Statistics. Suffice it to note that given the number of hours we spend toiling away on corporate terrain, the chances of stamping out the however-frowned-upon incidence of interoffice romance is as likely to happen as Janet Jackson taking the stage again on Superbowl Sunday. Simply put, it ain't gonna happen, because, rules notwithstanding, human nature will win out.

What it all comes down to is this: 44 percent of our civilian workforce is composed of unmarried people, working longer hours than ever before, according to a recent study by the American Management Association. It should hardly come as a surprise, therefore, that 59 percent of recently surveyed Americans reported having engaged in a workplace romance at some point (the discrepancy in numbers owing, in part, to extramarital affairs). For those dreamy romantics who fancy the happy ending (no pun intended) over the fiscal bottom line: nearly half of those workplace romances resulted in marriage or long-term relationships. Countless young soccer players, violinists, and paint-by-number aficionados would not have been born but for the fortuitous location of a network printer or office copier. Based on this data, it would be safe to assume that right now, at this very moment, there are some 20 million American workers eagerly awaiting a hot kiss in their inbox from somebody who sits very close by.

DSI is not suggesting, however, that we all drop our PowerPoints and go running into the next cubicle to pronounce our undying love. All we are saying is that if you happen to be in this situation, as lonely as it may sometimes feel, chances are you are not alone. Even under the best of circumstances, an interoffice romance can be fraught with social conflict, emotional strain, and professional hazard. A new relationship is hard enough to manage without the added pressures of work and secrecy adding to the mix.

We are people before we are employees. And no matter how much the corporate ethos idealizes separating emotions from work, we at DSI recognize that not only is that impossible, it's plain unhealthy. Nonetheless, we must learn how to create boundaries between our work and private lives, before our private lives disappear altogether. And we must honor our responsibilities in both spheres. If we do happen to find ourselves attracted to someone in the next cubicle or corner office, however, we should approach a relationship with prudence, caution, and above all else, respect for each other and the work environment.

FOLLOW-UP

In a one-year follow-up, DSI found Mr. Hornsby had used his generous severance package to cofound a small boutique advertising agency with a few other Golden Gaters who were "tired of being around that BOW" (i.e., Ms. Singer). His reputation as a creative dynamo has already required them to hire additional employees (none of then remotely attractive, as per Mr. Hornsby). Mr. Hornsby has also begun intensive therapy, and has made significant process. He is also taking a novel-writing class, where he's met a very attractive student, a few years his junior. He hopes that by the time the class ends, he will be ready to take the next step and ask her out for a latte.

After Mr. Hornsby's departure, Ms. Singer was brought up on charges of sexual harassment by the entire IT department and custodial staff, and is scheduled for termination without severance pending resolution of the trial. Her parents have prepared her old bedroom in North Philly in the event she must move back home, and contend that they are still very proud of their "little princess." Ms. Singer was able to convince a young attorney to take on her case, pro bono. She has not undertaken any therapy of any kind.

DO YOU SUFFER FROM NICEASS (NAUGHTY INTER-CUBICLE EXCHANGES AFFAIR SYNDROME AND SITUATION)?

If you suffer from seven or more of the following symptoms, consider yourself guilty as charged:

1. Sense of social isolation and strain in group meetings and social settings due to fear of exposing relationship through incriminating sidelong glances, suspicious body language, discomfort flirting with others, and oversensitivity to ribbing when romantic partner is present

2. Workplace "woodys," aka seat seepage, as a result of chronic arousal, also classified as desktop desire

3. An "understanding" with office housekeeping staff—often including cash gifts—after getting caught in compromised positions in the office supply closet

4. An escalating sense of confusion, disorientation, and discontinuity as a result of blurred professional/social/sexual boundaries

5. Secretive behavior regarded as "weird" by formerly friendly coworkers

6. Breakup anxiety about how it could impact professional relationship

7. Watercooler jealousy over how he/she interacts with other colleagues

8. Uncomfortable daily contact when relationship is new, undefined, or on the rocks

9. Increased pressure to dress well at work

10. Tendency to overanalyze company guidelines

11. Budding friendship with IT department in an effort to learn about company email monitoring

12. Added fears of public speaking when sexual partner is present

DSI MOST WANTED FUGITIVE

WANTED FOR:

INFIDELITY; COMPROMISED MORALS; DOUBLE STANDARDS WITH REGARD TO ACTS
OF BETRAYAL

Frederich Rupert Holmes, II

Aliases: Fred as a Doornail; Fred the Zed; Blight of the Living Fred; Better Fred Than Dead; Frederich the Grate

DESCRIPTION

Date of Birth: 1974

Place of Birth: Amherst, MA

Height: 6'2"

Weight: Approximately 170

Build: Lean/fit

Hair: Dirty blonde

Eyes: Blue

Complexion: White

Sex: Male

Nationality: American

Occupation: Private investor

Remarks: Mr. Holmes is an RDB (Rich Deadly Bore,) a man whose physical appearance and social standing draw women like flies only to leave them clamoring for insect re-pellant. He is articulate, nice looking, and allegedly searching for a wife of "good social standing" who will follow in his mother's footsteps and turn away from a distinguished career to raise a family and host charitable functions. He is regarded as particularly lethal for his apparent desirability, causing intelligent, right-minded women to blame themselves, fall into serious depression, and waste months to years of their lives in the process.

Scars and Marks: Mr. Holmes has a slightly bluish pallor, most evident under fluores-cent lighting. No other identifiable marks have been noted, other than a peculiar habit of wearing Brooks Brothers suits every day of the year, despite the fact that he undertakes very little in the way of business.

CAUTION

MR. HOLMES HAS CAUSED NUMEROUS SUCCESSFUL, INTELLIGENT WOMEN IN THE NEW ENGLAND REGION TO SUFFER STATES OF SEVERE CLINICAL DEPRESSION, WHO, TO THIS DAY, DOUBT THEMSELVES AND FEAR THAT HE WAS, AS HIS PARENTS PURPORTED, "THE PERFECT GENTLEMAN." MR. HOLMES HAS BEEN DEEMED A SEVERE PSYCHOLOGICAL HAZARD.

THIS INDIVIDUAL IS CONSIDERED EXTREMELY DANGEROUS AND UNFIT FOR GENUINE HUMAN INTIMACY.

IF YOU HAVE ANY INFORMATION CONCERNING THIS PERSON, PLEASE CONTACT YOUR *LOCAL DSI OFFICE*

REWARD

The Greater New England Chess Society is offering a reward of $200,000 for the capture of Mr. Holmes for his fraudulent portrayal of heroism and success as a master chessman in his efforts to ensnare women into dating situations.

EIGHT:

STICKY FINGERS

THE CASE OF THE RELATIONSHIP
TORN BY PORN

THE DSI 911

Margaret Ringold phoned the DSI hotline in a teary rage one Friday night at 11:52 P.M., reporting an increasingly common complaint among DUPEs. "I was already asleep when this loud grunting noise woke me up. I ran into the other room and there was that lame-ass sitting in front of his computer with a fistful of soppy paper towels, only two hours after he turned me down for sex for the fourth consecutive night claiming he was too tired!"

PRELIMINARY DIAGNOSIS

Team DSI assessed that the ARSE in this case, one Marc Berlucci, was suffering from PAWS (Pornography-Addictive Web Syndrome). This is commonly marked by such symptoms as a strong interest in pornography (*Jenna Jamesonitis*); an acute inability to distinguish reality from mediated fantasy; an expertise regarding current trends in breast augmentation complemented by strong preformulated opinions on which actresses have implants; and a working knowledge of labial pigmentation, genital waxing, and piercing locales. This disorder, while not an untreatable addiction, has the potential to negatively impact dating and relationships when men use porn as a "shorthand," so to speak, for meeting their sexual needs in lieu of engaging in actual intimate relations with their partners.

PARALLEL CASE ANECDOTALS

"When I first met Steve, he seemed so sweet and innocent. But then I found a cache of dirty DVDs and porn websites on his computer, and it was very hardcore stuff. I don't feel like I know who this guy is, and I'm also not sure if I can live up to the visions he now has of sex."

—Monica, 30

"Sure, I look at porn every now and again. What guy doesn't? I'd rather share it with my girlfriend, but she thinks my habit is disgusting. What she doesn't seem to grasp is that it could be a very erotic shared experience, and a prelude to great sex."

—Brian, 29

"Listen I'm open to trying new things, which includes enjoying erotic materials. But what bothers me is that he just goes into the den with his computer and closes the door. I want in on the fun, with him. I think that's what makes men and women different. We can enjoy porn as part of an overall sexual experience, but guys can just disappear into it."

—Serena, 32

"Guys who learn their sex skills from porn don't have a clue how to satisfy *real* women. It's like having sex with the Harlem Globetrotters—a lot of twirling and tossing, but no real sense of the art of lovemaking. It's all for show."

—Daphne, 27

"I'm definitely looking for the right woman, but for the time being I'm perfectly fine on my own. I've gotten pretty into Internet porn lately, and I have an extensive archive of women to keep me happy until I meet someone I want to have a real relationship with. The trouble is the women I find myself sexually attracted to lately are not the kind of women I would want to date in a serious way."

—Jon, 34

CASE SPECIFICS

The Dupe: Margaret Ringold
Age: 28
Location: Chicago, IL
Occupation: Nurse
Hair: Blonde
Eyes: Blue
Height: 5'5"
Weight: 135

RELATIONSHIP RAP SHEET/EX FILES

Past Serious Relationships: 3
Total Number of Sexual Partners: 4
Exes Still in Contact: 3

Interpersonal Infractions

February 1998

During her first sexual relationship, she always made her boyfriend turn the lights off during sex. Even after several months, Ms. Ringold refused to take baths or showers with him and wouldn't let him see her naked, always wearing lingerie during sexual encounters.

April 2001

Never opened a vibrator she received at a friend's bachelorette party despite a nagging curiosity to try it. Afraid her boyfriend might find it and ask to use it on her, Ms. Ringold finally gave it to a more sexually adventurous friend, deeply regretting it afterward.

2002–2003

Felt too self-conscious about her body to be on top during sex in her first two serious relationships. Continues to suffer from insecurity regarding how her body looks during lovemaking, which often prevents her from achieving orgasm.

Mating Misdemeanors

December 1997

Snooped through her boyfriend's desk to find out what he was "really up to." When she found the remainders of a dime bag of pot, she confronted him, saying, "If you did this without telling me, who knows what else you're up to!" The boyfriend, who was well aware of his girlfriend's less than liberal views on drugs, apologized, assuring her that he had nothing at all to hide, but had been afraid to jeopardize her opinion of him based on a stupid, infrequent high school habit. Ms. Ringold flushed the weed down the toilet and told him, "From now on, I'm going to check your pockets and desk drawers to make sure you're not hiding anything from me, because you've undermined my trust." The boyfriend meekly agreed, and started hiding his stash in a friend's dorm room instead, figuring it was easier that way.

May 2001

After months of cajoling, Ms. Ringold finally acquiesced to her boyfriend's desire to have a threesome with an Israeli exchange student they both knew, who was very comfortable with her bisexuality. On the night of the planned interlude, Ms. Ringold walked into the room an hour past the appointed time, saw her boyfriend and the other woman sitting several feet apart from each other drinking beer, and burst into tears, saying, "It's obvious that you guys are really into each other and that this has nothing to do with me. So why don't you go have sex and leave me the hell out of your disgusting deviant fantasies. I can't believe I gave you my flower!" Her boyfriend ran after her, saying he never meant to pressure her into doing something she didn't want to do. But Ms. Ringold broke up with him, citing "irreconcilable moral differences."

Flirtatious Felonies

March 2003

Went to Club Med Guadeloupe, and engaged in a torrid three-night affair with "Santos the surf instructor," with whom she was able to "be a different person." Knowing she was unlikely to see him again, she was totally uninhibited, swam naked in the ocean and had sex under the stars. "It was incredible. I told him what I wanted, and he did it. I didn't feel guilty about how long I took or worry about what he thought about my body or "smell," I was like a wild woman. I couldn't get enough. It was the most intense sexual experience I've ever had. I only wish I could have shared it with someone I truly love."

Psychographic Thumbnail

Ms. Ringold was raised in Wisconsin by politically conservative parents. From an early age, she felt self-conscious about her body and uncomfortable talking about sex. Despite being told by friends and family that she was very attractive, she was conflicted about being thought of as "sexy," given her parents' pejorative views of "promiscuous" (i.e., premarital) sex. Although of normal weight, she became convinced she was fat after puberty and went off to a "fat camp" before her first semester of college, which gave her somewhat more confidence in her appearance, but also fed into a lingering insecurity about her weight.

Ms. Ringold did not have any boyfriends until she attended the state university, where she was stunned to discover how relaxed other students were about sex, drinking, and drugs. After several months with her first boyfriend, she finally agreed to have sex with him, assuming the two of them would be married after graduation. After she learned of his minor pot-smoking habit, however, she grew distrustful. He became annoyed by her "uptight" refusal to experiment sexually and be naked in front of him. Throughout the relationship, Ms. Ringold's record indicates repeated instances of failing to reach orgasm and refusing to tell her boyfriend what he could do to make her come. She also withheld sex on numerous occasions as a form of punishment.

After terminating an eight-month relationship with a misogynist who wouldn't reciprocate her oral generosity, Ms. Ringold experienced her first truly uninhibited, sexually gratifying tryst with a man she met on vacation on a three-night stand. This made her more aware of her sexual potential and inspired her to become more open and experimental in her next relationship so she could enjoy that kind of sexual intensity with someone she loved.

Her decision to take a nursing job in Chicago reflected her desire to leave behind her family's restrictive values and figure out who she was in a more progressive, urban setting. She considered dating a man as sexually forward as Mr. Berlucci a positive sign of her own sexual r/evolution. She met Mr. Berlucci in the hospital emergency room, after he suffered a fractured ankle during a strip club squabble. At first Ms. Ringold was put off by his requests to have sex with the lights on, but eventually she grew to like it. As she spent more time with Mr. Berlucci, she developed a greater desire to "experiment." However, due to insecurity about her body, Ms. Ringold found Mr. Berlucci's clear admiration of porn stars, whose pictures decorated his computer screen, disconcerting. Rather than explain why the images made her uncomfortable, however, she told him that his preoccupation with porn was "revolting" and "degrading to all decent women."

While Ms. Ringold has grown somewhat more comfortable with her body and sexuality, Mr. Berlucci still contends that Ms. Ringold is "puritanical and judgmental," but believes that underneath it she's a "wild animal." To her marginal credit, Ms. Ringold has no record of ever faking orgasm with a partner to date, but has been known to rub it in a guy's face when she doesn't have a good time. She is very much in love with Mr. Berlucci, despite his "vile addiction to porn," and is hoping to find a way to make it work with him. "Aside from his disgusting fixation on simulated hooches, I find his companionship more and more delightful and comfortable every day. I wish I could just show him, once and for all, that watching all those dirty images is turning him into a gross pervert."

The Arse: Mark Berlucci
Age: 31
Location: Chicago, IL
Occupation: Commodities trader
Hair: Brown
Eyes: Brown
Height: 5'10"
Weight: 185

RELATIONSHIP RAP SHEET/EX FILES

Past Serious Relationships: 3
Total Number of Sexual Partners: >45
Exes Still in Contact: 9 (two are strippers)

Interpersonal Infractions

1988–2005

Has framed, autographed *Playboy* and *Penthouse* centerfolds hanging in his apartment covered in lipstick kisses that he obtained at the annual porn convention in Las Vegas, which he has regularly attended for years (up until this last year, when he went skiing with Ms. Ringold in Vermont instead). Often visits strip clubs with clients for "business meetings, at his bosses' request," and was removed from one such club for breaching the hands-off rule during a lap dance, which led to the squabble that landed him in the Chicago emergency room where he met Ms. Ringold.

Known to spend a fair amount of time in "VIP rooms," where he lets the good times and hundred dollar bills roll. On his thirtieth birthday, he and his buddies booked a suite in Las Vegas and ran up a $20,000 bill for "female entertainment."

Mating Misdemeanors

April 1993

While on spring break during his senior year of college, Mr. Berlucci and a half-dozen of his fraternity buddies went to Miami where they video-taped each other having sex with a variety of women at a popular club on the beach. Mr. Berlucci was so proud of his "performance" in the film that he made a habit of showing it to most of the women he slept with afterward, assuming they'd find it "hot" to see him "doing it with other babes." A few women he picked up at nightclubs agreed to have sex with him while the film was running, but a young attorney he was dating put an end to his fun by destroying the videotape before she left him in a fit of outrage.

March 2001

Mr. Berlucci sent a number of explicit digital pix to a woman he met on an adult-only Internet dating site, not realizing that the woman was his girlfriend's best friend. The girlfriend had set up Mr. Berlucci, sensing he was "up to no good," by planting spyware on his computer to track his whereabouts. After her best friend forwarded the photos, his girlfriend printed out hundreds of copies and mailed them to Mr. Berlucci's office. Mr. Berlucci was proud of the pictures and gave out autographed copies to all of the women at his firm.

Flirtatious Felonies

January 2002

While at an industry conference in Las Vegas, Mr. Berlucci cheated on his second "girlfriend," a high school art teacher "with a hot rack," whom he'd met at a local diner. The girlfriend called to check up on him, and he picked up his cell phone and told her he was too busy to talk. When Mr. Berlucci returned from the weekend, she confronted him and asked what he'd done while he was away. He told her that he'd had a fabulous time and had sex with two 36D blond prostitutes. Not expecting an honest answer, the girlfriend was dumbstruck and asked, simply, "How could you do this to me?" Mr. Berlucci replied, "We've only been dating a few months and we never said we were monogamous. Besides, it has nothing to do with you. I've had this fantasy for a long time, and I expect you to respect that." The girlfriend, to her own amazement, did not break up with him immediately owing to his honesty, but realized soon after this was not a man she would want to marry and eventually left him for another man. Mr. Berlucci was, surprisingly, disappointed and realized he wanted a companion in his life.

Psychographic Thumbnail

The youngest of three boys, Mr. Berlucci grew up in a middle class neighborhood in Cleveland. His father, a successful plumber, took over his own father's business, which he expected his sons to do as well. His mother prided herself on being what she called "a modern old-fashioned girl," a wonderful cook, a devoted homemaker, and "a hot tamale in the boudoir." Mrs. Berlucci has a tolerant view of her husband's preoccupation with pornography and strip clubs and does not begrudge him an occasional trip with his lodge buddies to Vegas for gambling and "what not." However, Mr. Berlucci is careful never to let Mrs. Berlucci see his porn collection, which he says is "distasteful and inappropriate for a wife and mother." Mrs. Berlucci understands that appearance is important to her husband and has worked very hard to keep her figure, exercising around an hour a day. For her thirty-fifth birthday, Mrs. Berlucci was given a boob job (primarily for her husband's pleasure) and an ice cream cake shaped like breasts. The couple retired to their bedroom early.

The boys, each three years apart, got into the normal run of skirmishes, but were very close knit, sharing a love of hockey, vintage cars, and porn, thanks to their father, who generously shared his stash with his sons from an early age. On Mark's sixteenth birthday, he was taken by his father and two brothers to a strip club, a family tradition, one which Mrs. Berlucci accepted with feeble reproach. Mr. Berlucci told his son to take a look around and "find the babe with the hottest pair of tits." The four Berlucci men spent a fair amount of time making comparisons, which involved several table dances along with a few lap dances for the senior Berlucci. When Mark found the girl with the largest breasts, Mr. Berlucci shoved two hundred dollar bills in her hand and said, "Take my youngest son to the back room and make him a man." During the next fifteen minutes, Mr. Berlucci received his first blow job and also lost his virginity, which he later reported "all went by so quickly I could hardly remember it." When he returned, however, the three older Berlucci's applauded, his father remarking: "Now you're one of us."

Of the three boys, only Mark went to college and moved out of state, the other two carried on the family plumbing business. Mr. Berlucci still goes home every Christmas and Easter and is considered the smartest of the bunch. Although they miss him, they are very proud of his professional success.

Mr. Berlucci has largely engaged in one- or two-night stands, and has had only three serious girlfriends to date, only one of whom he has attempted to remain faithful to, that being Ms. Ringold. His first girlfriend, an attorney he met soon after he graduated from college, broke up with him when he asked her to have sex with him while watching a video of him having sex with other women. He did not mourn her loss. The second girlfriend, some years later, enjoyed Mr. Berlucci's energy and healthy sexual appetite, but decided she could not see a future with him and broke up with him for a teacher like herself, having grown weary of his juvenile sexual antics. Mr. Berlucci then realized how much he wanted a long-term partner.

Ms. Ringold and Mr. Berlucci have now been dating for four and a half months, and Mr. Berlucci is proud that, other than a handful of lap dances and some time spent in Internet chat rooms, he has managed to stay "faithful" to her. He is drawn to her "smokin' bod and big naturals [boobies]," along with her prudish nature and nurse's uniform. As Mr. Berlucci reported to an undercover DSI agent posing as a stripper: "I know that underneath that prim exterior there lurks a wild animal. She's everything I ever wanted in a woman all rolled into one. She's sexy and clean and everything in between. I think she's the one, but I guess I have a hard time staying focused on just one woman. . . . So, how much for a lap dance?"

RELATIONSHIP RECONNAISSANCE

Mr. Berlucci and Ms. Ringold met while Ms. Ringold was on duty at Chicago General Hospital. Mr. Berlucci entered the emergency room with a fractured ankle following "an incident with a bouncer at a strip club," he told Nurse Ringold, without any hint of embarrassment. He later claimed that he liked "her naughty nurse's uniform" and was impressed with her "ability to care for him." Mr. Berlucci secured her phone number, and called her two weeks later, suggesting that they grab "dinner and a movie." Mr. Berlucci's choice of film, *Love Actually*, immediately suggested a proactive romantic intention. Ms. Ringold was smitten from the beginning and loved Mr. Berlucci's physical strength, high energy, and domineering personality, although she told friends she found his confidence a little intimidating. While he often commented admiringly on her "tight little ass," Ms. Ringold could not fail to notice him gawking at other women.

The couple had sex for the first time on their third date, after a Mexican meal involving several rounds of margaritas. Mr. Berlucci was very attentive to Ms. Ringold's sexual needs during the first three months of their relationship, although she often had this odd feeling she was being watched. She told DSI: "He always seemed like he was performing or putting on a show." Nonetheless, he was very focused during their liaisons and exhibited no reservations about going down on her. Whenever she apologized for "taking so long," he'd reply: "The longer the better. There's no place in the world I'd rather be," which was exactly the kind of reassurance Ms. Ringold needed to kick back and enjoy. While his desire to have sex with the lights on—"I want to see *everything*"—was ini-

tially met by Ms. Ringold with significant trepidation, his persistent rein-
forcement of her beauty and sexiness enabled her to "take a deep breath
and give it a shot." She was committed to becoming that person she'd
seen a hint of during her three-night stand. Soon, she was also reveling in
lights-on sex and even sneaking a glimpse up at the mirrored ceiling without searching for flab or sag.

After four months, however, Mr. Berlucci started to lose sexual interest in her, marked by a slow decrease in sexual activity. Unbeknownst to
Ms. Ringold, this coincided with a conversation he had with his parents:
"I met the girl I'm going to marry. She cooks, she cleans. She even has big
boobs!" after which, Mr. Berlucci felt nauseous, worried that she was too
much like his mother. When Ms. Ringold questioned his sexual slow-
down, Mr. Berlucci remarked that he was "stressed out from work" without mentioning his secret plan to pop the question on her next birthday,
less than two months away.

Ms. Ringold had, meanwhile, experienced a sexual reawakening of
sorts and was more eager than ever to have sex and try new things with
Mr. Berlucci. She even suggested watching porn together or going to a
strip club, which she remarked "are obviously totally disgusting, but I
would do since I know you like them." Mr. Berlucci adamantly declined,
saying, "a lady like you has no business watching that kind of filth or going to that sort of place," whereupon he turned her over onto her hands
and legs, had very quick sex with her, called her a "wet-pussy cock-
sucking whore," and passed her a vibrator, running to the bathroom afterward, sick with guilt, for having defiled the future mother of his
children.

When queried by Ms. Ringold as to why he was repeatedly turning
down sex with her and what he was doing behind closed doors on his
computer, his response was, "nothing, just work stuff." Ms. Ringold long
suspected he was hiding something: "I know he's lying because his eyes
dart back and forth, and he starts gulping. And he's sometimes out of
breath when I bring him lemonade and home-baked cookies. A few
times, when I tried to sit on his lap, he sort of pushed me away, like he
didn't want me to know something was *up*, so to speak." I guess I'm

mostly hurt that he didn't want to share this with me. I know that it's taken me a while. And while I would never do anything absolutely immoral and disgusting like have a threesome or do a pornographic video, I really do want to be more open and experimental. I guess the funny thing is, now that I want to be dirty, he wants me to be clean!

DATE SCENE RECONSTRUCTION

Liaison One: My Brown-Haired Girl

LOCALE: Mr. Berlucci's living room

Synopsis: During a routine weekend evening, Mr. Berlucci asked Ms. Ringold to dress up in her nurse's uniform, along with fishnet stockings, stripper-type stiletto heels and a brown wig, giving her the appearance of a completely different woman. He had also procured metal handcuffs. Mr. Berlucci then asked her to pretend he was a police officer bringing her in for improper nursing etiquette. While Ms. Ringold agreed to the ruse, she did not completely surrender to the submissive role-playing, threatening, instead, to put the handcuffs on "Officer Berlucci" and give him a thorough physical exam. The couple had a blow-out argument, with Ms. Ringold stating that he was too controlling about what they did in bed, accusing: "You always have some disgusting porn scene you want to play out." Mr. Berlucci replied: "You didn't even try my fantasy. You ruined everything." Ms. Ringold did not spend the night, choosing instead to retire to her own apartment. Mr. Berlucci spent the rest of evening viewing online porn of women getting dominated and fell asleep after masturbating three times.

Witness Testimony: The clerk at the adult toy store who sold Mr. Berlucci the heels and stockings noted that he "must have one hot lady," waiting at home, cautioning him: "The cuffs and bondage gear work better if they're not a surprise, since, when it comes to B&D, you never know what side a woman's bread is buttered on."

Liaison Two: Motel Six(ty-nine)

LOCALE: The Skyway Motel, I-94

Synopsis: While driving to Milwaukee to visit Ms. Ringold's family, she and Mr. Berlucci stopped for the night at a roadside motel. The late seventies-era motel room (complete with ceiling mirror and a vibrating bed) resembled many of the porn videos Mr. Berlucci had seen, and he begged Ms. Ringold to let him videotape their liaison, suggesting that it was for private use only. Mapping out several classic porn scenes, he seemed more interested in the footage than he was in his partner. Ms. Ringold, however, found the room filthy and "disgusting" and did not want to be naked on the bed. Moreover, she was not comfortable with the videotaping, partially because she was worried she would look heavier on video. The conversation soon erupted into an argument with Ms. Ringold asking, "Why do you always have to turn everything into a revolting dirty video. Why isn't just having sex with me enough?"

Witness Testimony: The night clerk noted that "the totally hot babe" seemed unhappy with the accommodations from the moment she walked into the lobby/bowling alley. Mr. Berlucci had asked for the honeymoon suite, which was the fanciest room in the motel complete with a hot tub, but it was unavailable.

Liaison Three: Three's Company

LOCALE: The Voodoo Lounge

Synopsis: Mr. Berlucci arranged for a "surprise" threesome with a friend of his named Rayne, a woman Mr. Berlucci later claimed to have met through work (who DSI has since determined was a professional stripper whom Mr. Berlucci had received paid blow jobs from twice before). Mr. Berlucci and Ms. Ringold showed up at the bar and had a few drinks. An hour or so later a sexy woman in a short miniskirt with several tattoos and a belly ring came over to Mr. Berlucci, claiming she was "meeting friends" who had just "bailed on her." Being a polite Midwesterner, Ms. Ringold asked her to join them. Several rounds later, Rayne began caressing Ms. Ringold. When Ms. Ringold asked what she was doing, Rayne replied, without thinking: "Mark thought we'd like each other." Ms. Ringold stormed out of the bar and demanded an explanation. When Mr. Berlucci admitted his plan, Ms. Ringold stated: "I told you already that I am not interested in having a threesome. How dare you set me up like that? There are many things I would be happy to try with you. Why must you insist on getting me to do something I don't feel comfortable with or excited about? Don't you want me to enjoy sex too, you vile porn boy?"

Witness Testimony: According to the bartender at the Voodoo Lounge, Mr. Berlucci paid him extra to pour strong drinks, saying "he wanted to loosen up his girlfriend for a potential three-way. He offered me a fifty, but I didn't take it. I told him to watch it, that a man's fantasy can be a woman's fear. And that his girlfriend was super hot and any guy would be happy to take her off his hands if he wasn't careful."

FORENSIC ASSESSMENT AND EVIDENTIARY ANALYSIS

Physical Evidence

Mr. Berlucci's Online Habits

A code-level sweep of Mr. Berlucci's home and work computers, revealed that he spent several four- to seven-minute blocks of time a day viewing porn online, often when Ms. Ringold was cooking dinner or waiting for him to come to bed. Our analysis provided a "digital footprint" that allowed us to make the following assessment:

➤ Several subscriptions to mainstream porn sites, including Vivid Girls and Hustler's Barely Legal

→ A strong presence on several amateur sites, including hornywives.com and multiple hits to a Japanese "ass fetish" site

→ Visits to fetish sites and BDSM communities, but only as a temporary "lurker"

→ The presence of a browser washer, designed to cleanse his computer of visits to porn sites

→ Frequent instant messages from handles like "boobalicious" and "facialqueen" asking if he was free

Our investigation also noted that the ARSE spent a substantial amount of time engaged in behaviors that would seem to corroborate his testimony that he was simultaneously working and reading financial/business news:

→ Presence on several commodities trading websites, including a central role on one bulletin board devoted to brokers looking to start their own companies

→ Bookmarked sites pertaining to how to pick the perfect engagement ring and romantic honeymoon spots in the Caribbean

→ A recurring bill from BigBalls.com initially was considered in the porn sweep. However, further scrutiny reveals that Mr. Berlucci is in charge of procurement of equipment and other miscellaneous items for his basketball team, and BigBalls.com actually deals in sports equipment

Mr. Berlucci's Dwelling

Further investigation of his home revealed the following:

→ A large stock of porn DVDs divided by genres, i.e., big boobs, big butts, anal, threesomes, S&M, lesbian, etc.

→ Lubes, condoms, and a double-crown studded leather cock ring

→ Autographed photographs of *Penthouse* and *Playboy* models hung throughout his apartment; several signed Polaroids of Mr. Berlucci and various porn stars taken at strip clubs and Las Vegas with his bosses

→ Several female-friendly vibrators (including the ever-popular rabbit), indicating Mr. Berlucci's understanding of clitoral stimulation

→ A well-worn copy of *She Comes First: The Thinking Man's Guide to Pleasuring a Woman*

→ An email to his brother in which he declared his love for Ms. Ringold, but also his concern that his "sexual needs might not be met by her alone"

Ms. Ringold's Dwelling

While Mr. Berlucci was the suspect under investigation in this case, team DSI also examined Ms. Ringold's home to determine if there were countervailing indicators that might reveal further aspects of her purported sexual openness:

→ An examination of her bathroom revealed a large cache of condoms and other forms of birth control

→ Shower scrutiny revealed a tendency toward pubic grooming, but (based on follicle volume) not the fully shaved "landing strip" look that Mr. Berlucci urged her to emulate

→ A STUB (Sex Toys Under the Bed) analysis revealed the presence of two vibrators, both gifts from Mr. Berlucci, with dead batteries, indicating earlier excessive use (hence, the wild animal in her) and failure to replace the batteries (thus, an ability to "shut off" her sexuality altogether when angry, i.e., consistent with a propensity to withhold sex as a means of punishment).

SPARK Test

Because the DSI investigation yielded countervailing evidence, which suggested the issue may be relationship-oriented (as opposed to ARSE-specific), we conducted a SPARK Test. The results of the SPARK test led us to the following conclusions:

→ This relationship is not Dead Upon Departure (DUD)

→ There is a requisite amount of Highly Erotic Attractive Traces (HEAT) between Mr. Berlucci and Ms. Ringold

→ Ms. Ringold, while clearly more sexually open and adventurous than she's been in the past, still jumps to snap moralistic judgments that feed into Mr. Berlucci's madonna/whore complex, making him uncomfortable sharing some parts of his fantasy life with her, especially those regarding porn

→ The results indicated that the sexual relationship has potential, but needs to be worked on in a mature way, with less judgment, and more tolerance on both sides achieved through a deeper level of communication

DICK Test

Mr. Berlucci willingly submitted to a Determined Inability to Commit Kibbosh (DICK) test, which involved showing Mr. Berlucci nonsexually provocative photos of Ms. Ringold and utilized electrical probes and brain scans to determine his potential commitment capability. A high range of activity in the hypothalamus, limbic, and caudate nucleus regions of the brain indicates that Mr. Berlucci is free from major impediments to commitment and is inherently attracted to Ms. Ringold. It is clear that Mr. Berlucci wants to make the "leap to love," but feels uncomfortable sharing some parts of his fantasy life with Ms. Ringold, owing partly to her inclination to judge and partly to Mr. Berlucci's inability to integrate his desires for marriage with feelings of sexual arousal (without associated guilt/disgust).

KISS Index

A Kinkiness Indicator and Sensuality Sensor (KISS) Index indicated that Mr. Berlucci and Ms. Ringold scored equally high on the sexual thrill-seeking scale, with Mr. Berlucci achieving higher scores regarding fantasies involving typically pornographic scenarios to which he evidenced an immediate Pavlovian jolt of arousal (consistent with a mild PAWS symptomology), and Ms. Ringold getting a higher verbally cued score regarding role-playing scenarios and one-on-one encounters featuring multiorgasmic female pleasuring. As they are now moving from romantic love to the attachment phase in the mating cycle and natural sex stimulants are waning, these differences are becoming more apparent. Mr. Berlucci's arousal level is declining, owing to the absence of novel stimuli (owing to mild PAWS and external factors), while Ms. Ringold's desire has grown due to her increased comfort and desire to explore sexually with Mr. Berlucci.

DSI FINDING

DSI has determined that while Mr. Berlucci does, indeed, seem to have a significant case of PAWS, his "adjusted" behavior score is close to normal range, especially given his stress about making a lifetime commitment to Ms. Ringold and tendency to view women as either the kind you marry (his mother/Ms. Ringold) or the kind you desire (strippers, porn stars). While Ms. Ringold's suspicions were partially correct, the degree to which he suffers from PAWS was not as advanced as her initial call suggested. Furthermore, several mitigating factors were at play, including Ms. Ringold's habit of cloaking her likes and dislikes in moralistic language rather than admitting how her own insecurities feed into her judgments. This strident stance feeds into Mr. Berlucci's discomfort in sharing his pornographic interests with Ms. Ringold.

RELATIONSHIP REHAB

Having determined that the couple has the potential to succeed in a long-term relationship, we recommend the following:

- ➤ Mr. Berlucci should stop rushing toward marriage and consider undergoing short-term counseling to deal with his emotional and psychological fears and his unresolved issues regarding his parents' marriage.

- ➤ Mr. Berlucci should limit his use of erotic materials in order to reestablish trust with Ms. Ringold.

- ➤ Mr. Berlucci should make more of an effort to share his fantasies with Ms. Ringold and should try to engage in role-playing and other sensual, pleasure-based activities, which Ms. Ringold enjoys, while accepting that she might not share all his fantasies.

- ➤ Mr. Berlucci should stop frequenting strip clubs, and engage in more social activities with Ms. Ringolld that will deepen their mutual experience of couplehood.

- ➤ Ms. Ringold must not form snap moralistic judgments regarding Mr. Berlucci's fantasies, regardless of where they've come from.

- ➤ Ms. Ringold should continue to make an effort to show him her "tolerant, open, and experimental" side and not label everything that falls outside her lexicon of desire as "deviant" or amoral.

- ➤ More effort needs to be made by both of them to unite their respective "love-maps" and discover the dynamic points of convergence.

DATING DIAGNOSTIC

If a picture is worth a thousand words, then it's a wonder we can hear ourselves think. Sexual images of half-naked women and men blanket our billboards, buses, trains, magazines, TVs, products, laptops, cell phones, and the rest of the high-tech appendages of everyday life. We are constantly assaulted with visions of surgically enhanced, cosmetically altered, digitally "perfected" bodies that tell us beauty is in the eye of the beholder, subject to changing consumer trends.

Long gone are the days when a centerfold pinup was enough to hold our attention for the rest of the month. Adult videos and magazines boast more live footage, more money shots, bigger breasts, better threesomes, rougher anal sex, and nastier blow jobs. Internet portals offer dozens of streaming video clips, doctored up photos, and raunchy language all displayed on one convenient page, organized by age, ethnicity, oversized body parts, sex acts, to satisfy every fetish from animation to zoological intrigue. Why choose only one woman or sex act when you can enjoy them all at once? It's all part of a growing trend that we at DSI call Sexual Attention Deficit Disorder (SADD) disorder.

Easy, fast, and uncomplicated, Web women (and men) are always aroused, not prone to complain if we're too fast or slow on the trigger, or remind us beforehand that we forgot to load the dishwasher. They do not care about our penis (or breast) size or how much we earn in a year. They do not expect us to give them a general idea where the relationship is headed. We know exactly where it's headed, and we like it that way.

It should come as little surprise, therefore, that an estimated 40 million men regularly frequent Internet porn sites, with over 20 percent engaging in such behavior at the workplace. The adult industry currently releases 11,000 adult movies per year—more than twenty times that of mainstream movie production. According to a recent study, 42 percent of adults surveyed reported that their partner's use of pornography made them feel insecure, while 41 percent admitted they felt less attractive, based on the acts and images shown in their partner's pornography.

Viewing pornography (via the Internet or any other means) is not itself a disorder. It is only when the viewing affects other aspects of one's dating life and relationships that it becomes problematic. It only rises to the level of PAWS when masturbating to pornography becomes chronically chosen over sex with an available partner.

In some cases a man or woman may be driven toward porn by a sexless relationship with someone who is not meeting basic sexual needs. In such situations, the issue is generally not the porn per se, but a lack of connection and/or communication. The couple may have lost, or never had, the necessary SPARK (beyond the first throes of chemical attraction) or may have severely unbalanced sex drives that leave one partner chronically wanting more and the other feeling inadequate.

Another outcome of porn viewing is a situation where a couple has a shared interest in porn, and where the porn is integrated into the couple's sexual relationship. In this case, the couple watches porn together, so there is none of the secrecy and hiding associated with single male viewing. While women are traditionally less visually stimulated than men, many women do find they enjoy watching a little porn as a form of foreplay, especially when they themselves play an active role in the selection of the viewing materials. The only time this presents a problem is when the couple cannot get turned on without turning to auxiliary pornographic stimuli, hence forming a couple-based dependency.

In many cases, men with more intense porn-viewing behaviors than Mr. Berlucci do have actual addictions. According to a recent study by MNBC, 25 million Americans visit cybersex sites between one and ten hours per week, while another 4.7 million do so in excess of eleven hours. With more than 30 million new porn pages appearing on the Web each month, it should come as no surprise that more and more people are becoming "addicted to porn," which DSI would define as those who chronically choose porn-based sexual gratification over relationship-based sexual gratification with a partner, finding "real life" women and scenarios disappointing or insufficiently stimulating owing to a SADD. Their libidos have, effectively, been reprogrammed to respond to compound digital stimuli (as one would find on a typical Web portal) as opposed to ordinary real-time sex, complete with emotional intimacy and background noise (domestic responsibilities and pressures). These numbers are only growing. Like alcohol and drug dependency, addiction to porn requires treatment and counseling. Recovery requires a necessary period of complete withdrawal and a need to relearn how to focus the arousal process on real-life stimuli, rather than compounded overstimulation. Men who get lost in porn often have difficulty dealing with real women.

We each have a unique "love-map" (our sexual fingerprint that informs our fantasies, inhibitions, and sexual tastes). Some of us are high sensation seekers, while others take the low road. In general, people are sexually compatible when they're more evenly matched, be it at the high or low end of the scale. Differences in sexual compatibility often start to manifest when we move out of the infatuation phase (within the first year) and into the attachment phase (after a year or so), and we are no longer being fueled by potent sex chemicals, which enhance our sexual attraction.

Because such incompatibilities do not often become apparent until a relationship has been established, couples must work hard to overcome these discrepancies. This takes openness and communication.

Porn can be a necessary "gap-filler." When shared, couples can use the images as a starting point to explore their fantasies. Individually, porn can be a healthy way for a person to enjoy private self-pleasuring and discovery, while remaining a fulfilled person inside or outside a relationship. Basically, it's all about balance. When a person or couple comes to depend on such external visual stimuli as a trigger to arousal and ultimate gratification, it can become a dangerous substitute for engaging in more emotionally meaningful interactions.

Yet unless we are living in a cave (making procurement of this book unlikely), none of us can turn our backs altogether on the images society feeds us, which, whether we like it or not, form the tropes of our sexual attractions and desires. Rather than jump to moralistic judgments about the political correctness of our fantasies, we need to learn how to accept, embrace, and discuss the full spectrum of our desires with our partners, and harness their power for developing new and more creative sex scripts. Because that's all those images are—fantasy. As long as we don't confuse performance with actual behavior, porn is no different than anything else we view in the movies or on TV: it's relatively mindless, predictable entertainment. Being that it's entertainment, some of it we'll like, and some of it we won't. The most important thing to remember is: when it comes to porn, at the end of the day (or night), the boob tube should turn off so that we can truly turn on.

FOLLOW-UP

A one-year DSI follow-up found Mr. Berlucci and Ms. Ringold still together and very recently engaged. Mr. Berlucci has channeled much of his former interest in porn into developing a deeper erotic connection with Ms. Ringold. In fact, he has discovered that intimacy can be a turn-on in its own right, especially with someone as up for adventure and role-playing as Ms. Ringold. He also engaged in a brief course of individual counseling to help him isolate and resolve his fears of marriage and understand that he does not want the kind of relationship his parents have. Ms. Ringold has opened up somewhat to porn and found that some of it can be stimulating. Says Ms. Ringold: "Porn is a way of introducing new possibilities, but we definitely don't watch it every time we have sex or even leave it on the whole night. Nothing we see could ever be as intimate as what we dream up in secret all on our own." It has even helped Mr. Berlucci get more comfortable being dominated. Said Ms. Ringold, "Those handcuffs he bought? Well guess who's been 'getting arrested'? Mark still won't bend over for a full exam, but hey, you never know what the future holds."

DO YOU (OR A PARTNER) SUFFER FROM PAWS (PORN-ADDICTIVE WEB SYNDROME)?

If you exhibit thirteen or more of the following symptoms, consider yourself *guilty* as charged:

1. Porn usage interferes with the ability to function at work and home.

2. Porn is used to escape or numb feelings.

3. Excessive amounts of money are expended on porn.

4. An important relationship has been lost or jeopardized due to porn.

5. Viewing porn is often chosen over dating and other social activities with singles or, worse, over sex with a partner.

6. Porn-based masturbatory sessions satiate the desire for real-life sex.

7. Compares members of the opposite sex to characters in porn and consequently deems them unattractive/unsexy and not worthy of pursuing for a real relationship.

8. Suffers an intensified level of "sexpectations" to look and perform like a porn star.

9. Exhibits a tendency to fetishize individual body parts and sex acts over responding to a partner's needs.

10. Focuses on sexual arousal in lieu of genuine intimacy/desire.

11. Stresses the need for privacy for computer time.

12. Carefully erases Internet history and cookie cache.

13. Displays a sense of disconnectedness or disorientation during partner-sex.

14. Shows a sudden interest to perform types of sexual positions that deviate from the established relationship sex-script.

15. Exerts undue pressure on a partner to turn fantasy into action.

16. Displays willingness to take risks (legal or work-related) to view pornography.

If You Are Male:

17. A propensity to stereotype women as sexually responsive to any and all forms of sexual stimulation without regard to the physical mechanics of female orgasm.

18. Experiences premature ejaculation and/or only desires stimulation of the head of the penis (because porn allows a viewer the ability to fast-forward to scenes of intense sexual excitement, it often reinforces an accelerated process of arousal).

19. Suffers from erectile disfunction due to performance anxiety.

20. Fixated on how own penis size compares to others.

21. Has an interest in Viagra and/or other sexual stimulants.

22. Cannot tell an airbrushed body from a real one.

23. Cannot discern a real female orgasm from a screaming phony.

24. Believes that female pubic hair is an evolutionary throwback.

THE DUPE WHO DUPED HERSELF

DUPE Interview Session

A policy change at the Federal Bureau of Intimacy has allowed DSI to release previously classified information from interrogations of ARSEs and DUPEs. As the following (unabridged) testimony reveals, the DUPE is occasionally determined to be a complicit party, although this is generally not known until sometime later in the investigation. Below is one in a long line of such cases.

File Name: I Keep Meeting the Wrong Guys
Date of Interrogation: August 9, 2003
DUPE Profile: Melanie Kotter
Age: 33
Location: Los Angeles, CA
Occupation: Talent agent; movie buff
DSI Disorder: Cannot get past a first date/claims to be dating the "wrong" types of guys; oversubscribes to a celluloid vision of Hollywood romance

Circumstances of Interrogation

When DSI first received Ms. Kotter's call, we thought maybe she'd just had a run of bad luck. During preliminary fact gathering, however, DSI discovered that while certain reported behaviors were, indeed, consistent with objectionable ARSE antics, most appeared a direct consequence of her own doing. Pursuant to standard procedural guidelines, Ms. Kotter was brought into DSI headquarters for voluntary questioning. What follows is a transcript of this interview.

Interrogation Transcript

DSI: We often find these background interviews yield valuable evidence leading to the apprehension of guilty parties, so we thank you for taking the time to come down and speak with us. In your original complaint, you told DSI dispatch, and I quote, "No matter what I do, I can't seem to meet the right men."

Kotter: Yeah, that's right. I always seem to wind up with total slime shooters or guys who aren't nearly as good as they crack themselves up to be.

DSI: Before we discuss the cases of actual malfeasance, why don't you tell us about the instances of false representation?

Kotter: I don't know. Some of them, it turns out, color their hair or dress in a way that disguises that they have back fat or potbellies. And others, well, even though they're wearing expensive clothes, when I check their labels, it turns out they bought them on sale and probably don't earn a lot of money. It's not that I'm so picky or anything. It's just that at this stage in my life, I'm really looking for Mr. Right.

DSI: Ms. Kotter, do you color your hair?

Kotter: Yes, but that's normal for women. *Gentlemen Prefer Blondes.*

DSI: And do you choose clothing that tends to camouflage those particular aspects of your figure that you might personally deem less than ideal?

Kotter: What, are you saying I'm fat or something? I'm just healthy. *Real Women Have Curves.*

DSI: Do you ever wear padded bras, control-top pantyhose, plumping lip-gloss, or concealer such that an interested party might have reason to assume you would look somewhat different, say, right out of a morning shower?

Kotter: Look, I'm in the industry. I get your drift. Stop playing the BS *L.A. Story.*

DSI: And should we assume that you purchased your Marc Jacobs bag and Hermes scarf at full price?

Kotter: Are you crazy? I shop the outlets, but I still expect *Breakfast at Tiffany's*.

DSI: Let's move on. When was the last time you were in a serious relationship?

Kotter: Well, I guess, not since college. The year after graduation I broke up with a guy I thought I was going to marry. I guess it was a case of *Irreconcilable Differences*.

DSI: Please explain.

Kotter: Well, we met at UCLA Film School. He was from New York and decided to go back home to do low-budget artsy crap. Man, what a waste of good earning potential. Anyway, he got some idiot production job at a nonprofit documentary studio in Brooklyn, while I landed a serious break as an unpaid intern for a children's talent scout. He wanted me to go live with him in New York for a while, but please. A Brooklyn nonprofit? So basically it was *Goodbye Girl* to me and that was that.

DSI: And you haven't been in a long-term committed relationship since?

Kotter: I've dated a lot of guys who had major potential, but like I said, I seem to wind up with either sleazy bastards or *Desperados*.

DSI: How would you describe the men you label sleazy bastards?

Kotter: Well, they have no interest in anything but a one-night stand or they're unavailable, you know like already living with someone. Or they're well-known cheaters. One was even *Just Married*.

DSI: And when you go out with them, are you aware they have partners or are inclined toward promiscuous behavior?

Kotter: Look, we all know the decent guys are already taken. But statistics prove that most of them will wind up back on the market at some point. As for the cheaters, people change, given the proper incentive. Anyway, it's worth an outside shot if the guy is really hot and loaded. Better than spending another Friday night *Home Alone*.

DSI: So, of the men you've gone out with who are single and seeking more than a casual encounter, have any of them asked you out again?

Kotter: I told you already. The only ones who want to see me again are total losers. That's *As Good As It Gets*.

DSI: How do you judge that?

Kotter: Well, mostly it's during a first date situation. They act too interested, if you know what I mean. They ask too many questions. They talk about what we might do on a second or even a third date, which is way over the top. They ask me what my hobbies are. It's weird. They're obviously pathetic, lonely clingers. Nobody else wants them. Why should I get stuck with them? In the last six months, I've gone out on maybe *50 First Dates*. And it's always the same ol' story: Either they're taken or they're losers.

DSI: How long are these first dates, typically, and what do they entail?

Kotter: Well, I don't like to have dinner, in case I decide to give 'em a toss. So it's usually drinks. Generally, it's around an hour or so before I decide whether they're "in" [makes air quotation marks] or definitely off the *Hook*.

DSI: And let me guess, the ones you like are the ones who are taken and the ones you don't are clingy losers.

Kotter: The rest are losers. Honestly, all it takes is a minute to know. I've got *The Sixth Sense*.

DSI: How do you typically meet these men?

Kotter: You know, at industry events, clubs, cocktail parties, sometimes through friends. But I try to avoid setups, since I usually wind up disappointing both the men and my friends on account of my high standards. I'm just not willing to settle. There have to be *A Few Good Men* still out there.

DSI: Do you feel that perhaps you are focused on the wrong qualities?

Kotter: No, not at all. I know what I like. And I'm self-confident enough to trust my *Basic Instinct*.

DSI FINDING

We marked this case unsolved pending further investigation under the classified heading: *What Women Want*?!??

This case was eventually placed in our "No identifiable ARSE" file, since no arrests were possible based on the information provided. The investigation led to a finding that Ms. Kotter was her own worst enemy, and that her lack of success had more to do with her skewed set of standards than anything the men she was dating were doing wrong. Further recommendations included forgoing all mainstream Hollywood movies for a period of six months while simultaneously viewing DVDs of the complete works of Ingmar Bergman.

NINE:

STUCK IN THE PAST

THE CASE OF THE MAN STILL HEXED BY HIS EX

THE DSI 911

The call came into the DSI emergency hotline from Sharon Yates one Thursday morning at 2:35 A.M. "My boyfriend just locked himself in the bathroom to console his ex-girlfriend again. I know her mother's sick and she needs someone to talk to, but why the hell does it have to be the man I'm dating?" While Ms. Yates was uncertain as to the precise level of involvement between them (due to the ARSE's refusal to respond to her "accusatory line of questioning"), she did not suspect outright infidelity. Instead, her concerns regarded his inability to separate himself emotionally from his ex. "Whenever he talks to her, he goes into another room and closes the door. When I ask him what they talked about, he tells me it's private and acts like I'm being paranoid, nosy, and jealous. I've tried to be understanding and respectful, but something about it smells fishy. Can a guy really be "just friends" with his ex-girlfriend? Or is he still hung up on her? What should I do? Oh shit, he's opening the bathroom door. Gotta dash!"

PRELIMINARY DIAGNOSIS

Based on DSI's vast ARSEnal of Ex Files, we have ascertained that this is a classic case of *Exus Cannotgetoverus*, marked by an overly friendly bond between former romantic partners. The disorder can range from a mild sense of nostalgia for the ex to a debilitating level of obsession, although most cases seem to fall somewhere in between.

When a serious relationship ends, it's natural to suffer a period of mourning for the loss of comfort, companionship, and common future goals. The situation presents a very different set of facts when the former couple, who may or may not be in new relationships, decides to engage in a "platonic" friendship, alleviating immediate feelings of loss to the detriment of proper closure. Very often the two exes reinitiate a connection with the sole intention of friendship, only to find that such reconnection triggers buried emotions leading to A-BUST (After BreakUp Sex Tryst). This behavior should not be confused with organic desire, since it is driven by an acute hormonal burst predicated upon an emotional, rather than sexual, need to re-create a familiar structure. Couples who break up and get back together often mistake this burst for deeper attraction and compatibility, sacrificing more meaningful relationships in the process.

PARALLEL CASE ANECDOTALS

"My most recent girlfriend used to question me all the time about my supposed feelings for my ex from college, whom I dated six years ago. I always told her she was wrong, but as it turns out, the ex from college and I got back together, a year after that last relationship ended. I guess I still had feelings for her after all. Luckily, so did she."

—Martin, 35

"Rebecca always claimed she was over her ex, and I believe that she was, but her ex was definitely not over her. He lived in a different state, but he was always sending her gifts and letters in the mail, and they had this flirty shorthand about music, movies, and people. She never did anything about it, but it was awkward. I felt bad for the guy, but it really started impacting our relationship. Eventually I felt like the outsider. She finally had to tell him to stop contacting her."

—Felix, 32

"Maddie is always questioning me about my exes and worrying about how she stacks up. 'Am I prettier than her? Is so and so smarter than me? Was she more adventurous in bed? Are you more in love with me than any of the others?' Blah, blah, blah. I used to actually try to answer her questions and reassure her, but now it just sounds like whining and it really gets under my skin. No matter what I do to prove she's the one, she can't stop obsessing about my exes."

—Mark, 28

"It's not that I still have feelings for Jack. It's just that what we had was really special—we were really young and innocent—and I guess I'll always have a soft spot for him."

—Serena, 32

CASE SPECIFICS

The Dupe: Sharon Yates
Age: 29
Location: Bethesda, MD
Occupation: Paralegal/part-time law student
Hair: Brunette
Eyes: Brown
Height: 5'3"
Weight: 119

RELATIONSHIP RAP SHEET/EX FILES

Past Serious Relationships: 8
Total Number of Sexual Partners: 8
Exes Still in Contact: 1

Interpersonal Infractions

1997–2003

Has a history of asking her boyfriends "too many questions" about former girlfriends; exhibits excessive fondness for looking through old photo albums containing pictures of previous partners and makes disparaging remarks how they're "not nearly as pretty as described." Often asks how she compares to an ex, with regard to physical desirability, breast size, weight, frequency of sexual interaction, and sexual techniques.

Feels no compunction about going through a boyfriend's personal belongings, including drawers, files, mail, email, and pockets, in order to ascertain whether he's "on the level" and can "be trusted." She considers this behavior justified by the fact that "most men are total dicks." Upon finding items that indicate potential cheating, she confronts them openly. If they express outrage at her invasive conduct, she says, "Yeah, well I guess I was right for not trusting you!"

Does not believe men are innately capable of fidelity, and believes a woman needs to protect herself and take preemptive measures to prevent unwarranted dalliances. She often sends friends to test her boyfriends at bars. In the event they flirt or make a pass, she proudly reveals that she planted a spy and will do so again, warning: "I'll be watching you, buddy!"

Will not engage in sex early on in a relationship, stating, "I know that's the only thing men want from women. So I make them wait for it."

Mating Misdemeanors

March 1999

After telling her boyfriend that she was "dying to meet" his ex-girlfriend, with whom he remained on friendly terms, the boyfriend set up a double-date. At dinner, Ms. Yates drank three margaritas and interrogated the ex as to how she managed the boyfriend's penchant for flatulence. Then she asked the ex's new boyfriend if it was true that the ex made ugly faces when she faked orgasm and if she really had small, flaccid nipples. The ex was so hurt that she never spoke to Mr. Hoffman again. Ms. Yates was openly delighted.

January 2001

Went into work late so she could inspect her boyfriend's apartment, picking the lock on his filing cabinet, where he kept all of his personal correspondence. Discovering a folder marked "Racy Stacy," she found dozens of dirty pictures plus printouts of recent emails. She scattered the pictures all over his bed with a note saying, "If you don't destroy these and block her from your email account, I will never see you again." She never saw him again.

Flirtatious Felonies

August 2003

Allowed an ex-boyfriend, who'd made a pass at her best friend, to help her move to a new apartment, accepting a housewarming present in the form of a Friedrich air-conditioner (which she allowed him to deliver and install in her fourth-floor walk-up), as "reparations for being a sleazy bastard." When the ex told her how sorry he was and how much he missed her, she said, "Too bad, so sad," and slammed the door in his face. The boyfriend was unaware of the fact that she had told her girlfriend to hit on him when he was drunk enough to "show his true colors."

Psychographic Thumbnail

Ms. Yates is the daughter of divorced parents. Her father left her mother when she was a toddler for someone "younger and more attractive," and then moved across the country to start a second family. While her father was responsible about paying child support and usually remembered to send a gift at Christmas and on her birthday (at his ex-wife's prompting), he never made any effort to remain an active part of her life. Ms. Yates wrote several letters to her father offering to go out West and meet the "rest of her family," but was told via her mother that it "wasn't a good idea."

Ms. Yates' mother, an attractive, petite woman who worked as a bookkeeper, had a number of boyfriends while Ms. Yates was growing up, but none of them seemed inclined to stick around. Ms. Yates told her daughter many times, "Men only want one thing. And after they get it, they move on."

Ms. Yates has a history of dating men who don't give her the respect she deserves. She has an elastic set of principles that lead her to accept flagrantly unacceptable behavior, which she assumes unavoidable, since "men are born liars and cheats," as her mother taught her. She works as a paralegal in a family law practice and plans to pursue a career as a divorce attorney after she graduates from law school so she can "nail those filthy bastards who think they can screw whatever they want, including their families."

Ms. Yates is often drawn to "bad boys" who put their friends first (bros before ho's), the kind prone to measure a woman's value by whether she's "doable." Ms. Yates seems to enjoy the level of antagonism these relationships engender, describing herself as a "ballsy bitch who doesn't take shit from assholes." As such, she frequently snoops behind their backs and interrogates them and their friends about suspected infidelity. Her low expectations inevitably bring the relationships to a dramatic head, never in her favor.

The longest relationship Ms. Yates has managed so far is eight months. Not interested in "one night stands," Ms. Yates refuses to have sex with her boyfriends for the first month "to keep them around." During this period, she is given to flourishes of self-confidence and demands of "proper treatment," such as being picked up and escorted home and taken to "classy restaurants and movies." But once sex enters the picture, she becomes paranoid and anxious, always searching for signs of betrayal. Owing to the men she chooses and her projected expectations, her suspicions eventually prove correct, which only strengthens her poor opinion of men.

The Arse: Bruce Hoffman
Age: 31
Location: Washington, DC
Occupation: Lobbyist
Hair: Brown
Eyes: Brown
Height: 5'10"
Weight: 185

RELATIONSHIP RAP SHEET/EX FILES

Past Serious Relationships: 5
Total Number of Sexual Partners: 21
Exes Still in Contact: 6 (only one of them is an actual former "girlfriend")

Interpersonal Infractions

1995–2004

Has had over a dozen "friends with benefits," with whom he has broken off communication upon being pressed to decide whether he was in love with them. The women are often stunned when he says he does not reciprocate their romantic feelings, having assumed there was "something more."

April 2000

Started "hanging out" with his best friend's ex-girlfriend, without asking the friend's permission or waiting for an appropriate interval of time. When the friend got wind and confronted Mr. Hoffman, he explained: "Look, I know you dumped her. It's not as if either of us was looking for something serious. We were just spending a little time together. She needed a friendly shoulder to lean on. She's really hurting now." When the aforementioned woman professed she'd "always had a thing for" Mr. Hoffman, he abruptly cut things off. When he told his friend what happened, mentioning in passing that she was not "all that good between the sheets," the friend took a pop at him, screaming, "I can't believe you treated her like a piece of common trash. She was really special to me. We were just going through a rough patch." Mr. Hoffman and the friend parted ways, and the couple eventually married.

Mating Misdemeanors

April 1997

Pursued a married woman under the guise of friendship, and later confessed his romantic feelings in a "handsy" manner over late-night drinks. When she informed him that she would not cheat on her husband despite the problems they were having (which she felt Mr. Hoffman had intentionally "exploited"), he became angry and called her a "cock-tease." The woman apologized for leading him on, whereupon he leaned over and tried to kiss her. Flabbergasted, she marched out of the bar, as Mr. Hoffman called after her: "No wonder your husband cheats on you."

March 2000

Invited several of his "friends with benefits" to his current girlfriend's surprise birthday party, hoping it might lead to a threesome. Two of the "special friends" stormed out in tears, unaware Mr. Hoffman had a girlfriend and that their relationship had been one of convenience rather than affection.

Flirtatious Felonies

March 2002

Called a woman he had been dating for several months by the wrong name in bed on numerous occasions. Frequently "blanks out" on his girl-friends' names and asks them to introduce themselves at parties. He attributes this to being "bad with names."

Psychographic Thumbnail

Like Ms. Yates, Mr. Hoffman was a product of divorce, although his parents remained on congenial terms after the split, living a few blocks apart to facilitate joint custody. The decision to break up was mutual—the result of a "dumb starter marriage right out of college." Mr. Hoffman's parents both remarried and started new families. On birthdays and holidays, they all get together, and everyone seems to get along without issue. Both his parents made demonstrable efforts to make him feel "special," often to the point of outright favoritism.

Mr. Hoffman's dating history is rife with "misunderstandings," based on his habit of developing close friendships with women that feature a "sexual component," but lack what he considers "true romantic spirit." Much like his parents, Mr. Hoffman believes that there is "only one ideal partner for each person" and that "fate has a way of bringing folks together when the time is right." He believes "It's just a question of keeping your eyes open. Sometimes true love can be sitting right under your nose without you even knowing it." Statements such as these have led his "friends with benefits" to suffer considerable emotional upset.

Prone to occasional swells of anger when his sexual advances are rejected, Mr. Hoffman has been known to accuse a naysayer of being "frigid" or "uptight" for not giving into passion regardless of consequence. He prides himself on his "evolved" views regarding women and sex and his ability to be open about his emotions and separate momentary lust from love-based desire.

His relationships are generally undefined, beginning as friendships and mutating into romantic attachments without him even realizing it. Upon becoming aware of a girlfriend's expectations of commitment, he makes a sudden assessment and usually breaks things off, figuring he would "know" if it was "true love." Afterward he starts to question whether he made a mistake, since "love can be sitting right under your nose without you even knowing it."

RELATIONSHIP RECONNAISSANCE

Mr. Hoffman and Ms. Yates met at a fundraising softball game to benefit children's social services. Mr. Hoffman liked the fact that Ms. Yates was athletic and outdoorsy, and was working her way through law school. He also admired her dedication to nailing deadbeat dads, a social ill he found similarly egregious. Ms. Yates was instantly attracted to Mr. Hoffman, as well as his desire to meet the right woman and start a family. A mutual friend who organized the event told Ms. Yates that Mr. Hoffman was single and had not had a "serious girlfriend for like two years." Another (male) mutual acquaintance said, "It was a bad breakup, since the two of them were friends before getting involved, but two years is enough time to get over anyone."

Their relationship started off slowly, under friendly terms. They went out several times with groups of people before Mr. Hoffman finally asked Ms. Yates out on a date. Ms. Yates was concerned that the social groups often included at least one of Mr. Hoffman's "special friends," but he was quick to reassure her that there was "nothing serious between them." His work as a lobbyist for the automotive industry took him to Detroit a good deal, and their first dates were spread out over a long period of time, leaving Mr. Hoffman blissfully unaware of Ms. Yates programmatic refusal to sleep with anyone in under a month. Both agreed that, above all else, they should be "friends."

Mr. Hoffman proved to be a good communicator and expressed his feelings of friendship and attraction to Ms. Yates often. She was not insecure about his feelings for her, but she was definitely put off by his many women friends with whom he'd slept. He explained that "there was nothing romantic between them," and none of them was "the one." He explained: "My parents always told me that the most important part of a successful marriage is friendship, and when I get married I want my wife to be my best friend as well as the love of my life." This reassured Ms. Yates that his intentions were honorable.

After four months of dating, Mr. Hoffman received an email from an ex he'd broken up with in Detroit two years earlier, after she'd insisted on knowing whether he was, in fact, in love with her. When he'd pronounced she was not "the one," she kicked him out onto the street, and he moved to D.C. They'd had no social contact for almost two years, until Mr. Hoffman learned from a mutual "friend" that she was engaged to another man. He suddenly became convinced she was "the one" and started emailing her under the guise of resuming their friendship. Then he met Ms. Yates. While his budding feelings for Ms. Yates diminished his sense of conviction about the ex, he remained unsure how he felt about either. Then two months into his relationship with Ms. Yates, the ex emailed him with two pieces of news: she had called off her engagement and her mother had fallen ill.

Mr. Hoffman began speaking to his ex with greater frequency after that point, explaining to Ms. Yates that he was trying to be a supportive friend in her "time of need." Ms. Yates felt obliged to accept this. Although she has tried to be understanding, she sensed a change in the tone of his voice when he spoke to his ex, and noted his habit of taking the phone into the bathroom to speak with her. Ms. Yates admits to DSI that she surreptitiously checked Mr. Hoffman's cell-phone log to determine the extent of their interactions, justifying her behavior by a need to protect herself. Mr. Hoffman recently told Ms. Yates that on his next work trip to Detroit he will stay an extra day to accompany his ex and her mother to the hospital. Ms. Yates feels that this behavior may be crossing a line. She believes he may have unresolved feelings for his ex, and is using the time with her to assess whether she is "the one." On the basis of such suspicions, DSI was able to expedite a wire-tapping warrant from the Federal Bureau of Intimacy. A subsequent VPA (voice pattern analysis) did reveal BTT (baby-talk tendencies) in the "this must be love" range. Openly confronting Mr. Hoffman with this discovery, he barked she was "out of line," and that he was simply trying to "cheer up an old friend."

DATE SCENE RECONSTRUCTION

Interaction One: Something Fishy

LOCALE: Ms. Yates's apartment

Synopsis: While cooking dinner together for several of Mr. Hoffman's friends, including a former "special friend" (all seated in the next room), Mr. Hoffman remarked: "Your kitchen is not as well stocked as other kitchens in which I've cooked." She let the comment pass while enjoying a glass of wine. Mr. Hoffman then added: "My ex Simone had a fondness for high-quality olive oils and artisanal cheeses." Ms. Yates bristled at the comparison, and suggested that if Mr. Hoffman liked her "oil and cheese so damn much," perhaps he should "go cook for her instead," huffing into the dining room to join their guests. Mr. Hoffman followed her, proclaiming: "You know, you could learn a few things from Simone. Frankly, I'm tired of attempting to doctor up your pedestrian paella and Chilean sea bass whenever we have guests." Ms. Yates proceeded to polish off the rest of the wine by herself without sampling a bite of the plebian culinary creations, leaving Mr. Hoffman to see the guests out and clean up alone.

Witness Testimony: Ms. Yates' dinner guests noted that Mr. Hoffman was rude to voice his objections to her cooking skills in front of company, but that it was true that her paella and sea bass lacked a "certain finesse."

Interaction Two: Can You Hear Me Now?

LOCALE: Mr. Hoffman's apartment

Synopsis: While snuggling in bed watching *Sliding Doors* one Friday night, Mr. Hoffman's cell phone rang. While he generally maintained a strict policy of "no phone calls during date night-in," he heard Simone's custom ring (the overture from *Carmen*). He quickly excused himself and shut himself in the bathroom with his phone. When he reappeared an hour and a half later, he explained that an "old friend was having a hard time." When Ms. Yates pushed him to admit it was Simone, he said simply, "So what if it is? I told you already, her mother his sick. Have a heart, for God's sake." Ms. Yates countered, "I thought she was engaged. Why can't she call her fiancé for emotional support?" Mr. Hoffman blurted out, "Because they broke up. . . . She's uhhh having a uhhh ttt-tough time." Ms. Yates asked Mr. Hoffman when he had developed a stutter, causing Mr. Hoffman to suggest Ms. Yates was "insane." Ms. Yates then demanded to see his cell phone bill. Mr. Hoffman refused, causing Ms. Yates to give him the "I'll be watching you" hand-to-eye gesture executed with characteristic aplomb by Robert DeNiro in *Meet the Parents*.

Witness Testimony: A neighbor with a wall adjoining Mr. Hoffman's bathroom said he heard what sounded like "shouts of joy" and "baby talk" during the hour and a half in question when Mr. Hoffman was on the phone.

Interaction Three: Chop Chop

LOCALE: The London Chop House, Detroit, MI

Synopsis: While in Detroit on business, Mr. Hoffman agreed to meet Simone for dinner to "make sure she was doing all right." He chose the best restaurant in the city, claiming it was on his "expense account." Ms. Yates was not apprised of the dinner plan, having been told by Mr. Hoffman that he was attending a "business function and would be back at the hotel late." Mr. Hoffman had earlier arranged for a bouquet of flowers to be sent to Simone, but claimed later to DSI investigators that these were for her sick mother [*Note:* A digital footprint of Mr. Hoffman's computer revealed that he sent daisies and carnations, consistent with a "get well" motif]. During the dinner, Simone spoke nostalgically of the "good old days" when they'd had so much fun together. Mr. Hoffman echoed her sentiments, failing to mention his relationship with Ms. Yates. The evening ended with the two vowing "never to lose touch again."

Witness Testimony: The maitre d' noted that Mr. Hoffman had requested "booth number one," aka the "proposal" table, which is secluded in a remote corner beside the fireplace. The valet who retrieved their respective cars commented that their goodbye hug seemed "extremely friendly" and noted that Simone was "a pretty good looker."

FORENSIC ASSESSMENT AND EVIDENTIARY ANALYSIS

Physical Evidence

An examination of Mr. Hoffman's dwelling reveals he is an avid "collector" and exhibits an overweening attachment to past relationships, as follows:

→ A well organized photo album devoted to his ex-girlfriends/special friends

→ A trove of letters, postcards, and birthday cards from family and ex-girlfriends, dating back to adolescence

→ Yearbooks from every academic institutions he attended, including elementary school

→ Books from various ex-girlfriends, including a copy of a Zen quote book from the ex-girlfriend in question, with the inscription "Just Breathe," signed, "Love always, Simone"

→ A wide musical collection focused on "chick music," including Nora Jones, Alanis Morissette, and The Indigo Girls

Past Relationship Assessment Test (PRAT)

The primary forensic tool deployed in this case was a PRAT, which uses magnetic resonance imaging of brain and heart-rate patterns to determine an ARSE's true level of interest in another party with whom he has had previous engagements. Mr. Hoffman's general PRAT suggested feelings of "warmth and tenderness," which, in and of itself, do not warrant alarm. However, Mr. Hoffman registered at warning levels with regard to his feelings of "protectiveness and concern," for Simone's well-being. During their farewell hug, a reverse regression pattern showed spiked norepinephrine levels, and heightened neurotransmission on dopamine pathways, indicating "advanced infatuation."

Florescent Infidelity Burner (FIB) Test

DSI administered a FIB to check for infidelity. Using a highly tuned infrared lamp, DSI undertook a thorough scan for traces of Simone's clothing fibers, scent, makeup, and other bodily fluids on Mr. Hoffman's person. While residue of Simone's perfume was found on Mr. Hoffman's suit jacket, such low levels of trace elements were deemed incidental to a public meeting. There was no evidence of physical infidelity, although Simone's heavy use of her signature perfume, Fracas, and her choice of a sheer Miu Miu peignoir over a La Perla camisole corset resulted in a high RAP (Romantic Attraction Potential) score on her part.

Suspicious Paranoid Insecure Ex Determination (SPIED)

Based on Ms. Yates's dating history, a SPIED was used to ascertain to what extent Ms. Yates' distrust of men may have contributed to her suspicions of Mr. Hoffman. It was found that while she engaged in behavior that exceeded appropriate bounds of privacy, she was justified in her belief that Mr. Hoffman had stepped over the line, with regard to his failure to disclose his level of contact with his ex and his conflict of allegiance.

DSI FINDING

While Mr. Hoffman exhibits many of the classic symptoms of *Exus Cannotgetoverus*, we find that his behavior stems more from an unrealistic perception of what "true love" is rather than an empirical attachment to his ex. Given his ability to be sensitive, open, and communicative and his laudable desire to marry his "best friend," we do not recommend termination of this relationship, but rather direct both parties to follow the guidelines set forth below.

RELATIONSHIP REHAB

DSI recommends partner probation, with the following specific conditions:

→ Mr. Hoffman must stop waiting for love to conk him on the head and realize that building a relationship conducive to marriage requires effort, patience, understanding, and serious commitment.

→ Mr. Hoffman needs to draw clear boundaries with his exgirlfriends, and accept that some behaviors are inappropriate and overly intimate, regardless of extenuating circumstances.

→ Mr. Hoffman needs to forge stronger bonds with Ms. Yates's friends and family, rather than cling to the extended families of past relationships.

→ Mr. Hoffman needs to be comfortable talking to his exes in the presence of Ms. Yates and avoid private or secret communications.

→ Mr. Hoffman needs to reassure Ms. Yates about his feelings for her.

→ Ms. Yates needs to accept that Mr. Hoffman has women friends, and that many of those women are likely to be attractive.

→ Ms. Yates needs to communicate her concerns rationally and constructively.

→ Ms. Yates must respect Mr. Hoffman's privacy.

⟶ In addition to the steps above, Ms. Yates should consider undertaking sessions with a cognitive therapist.

DATING DIAGNOSTIC

We all know the rule: "Never date someone on the rebound." But, as we get older, the chance of meeting someone single who is *not* on the rebound seems as likely as getting a great deal on a used car (without bargaining).

In this society of serial monogamists, most of us go from one relationship to the next with some degree of overlap. We date without committing. We commit while still dating. We leave ourselves open to *other* possibilities. In crude terms, we comparison shop. This culturally inscribed ethos to "keep looking" carries over into our long-term relationships. When we find ourselves at a difficult impasse, we tend to sniff around for something new *before* we end things. Then once the novelty of the new relationship fades, we have second thoughts. We fret over "the one that got away," and ponder "what might have been if only we knew then what we know now." And so we go back, or we rush forward, again and again. But at some point it has to stop, or else we wind up in a perpetual limbo between future and past without ever fully experiencing the present person in our bed.

Yet the question remains: how can we convince someone *else* to break the insidious cycle before we become the next "one who got away"? Such is the quandary for Ms. Yates.

Experience may make us wise, but it also leaves us wary. What makes dating so difficult as we get older is the number of disappointments, insecurities, and unspoken fears we bring to our relationships, based on the cultural tendency to get swept into new love without figuring out what went wrong the last time. While it's easy to blame a breakup on stock phrases like "the passion fizzled," "we grew apart," or "our long-term goals were incompatible," that doesn't help us understand how we contributed to those problems.

This lack of reflection leaves us guessing and worried. After all, if it happened before, it can happen again. But rather than focus on something as patently unpleasant as what made us fall out of love with someone we couldn't imagine living without, we take the shortcut and look for the familiar danger signs. Often it's our very compulsion to ferret out those patterns that causes us to replicate them all over again.

Still, there comes a time when we have to move on. Even though we may not be done sorting out our feelings from the past, we need to focus on what we're trying to build in our new relationships. While it's good to maintain connections with people who have shared important fragments of our lives, there are limits. We cannot create a future while gazing at the past and ignoring the present. Perhaps the best we can do is realize we weren't perfect then and we won't be again, and do our best to approach each new relationship with an open mind and fresh heart.

FOLLOW-UP

Despite early success, Mr. Hoffman broke up with Ms. Yates six months after our investigation to pursue a relationship with Simone, still convinced she was "the one." Four months later, he called Ms. Yates from Simone's bathroom to tell her that Ms. Yates was, to the best of his knowledge, the love of his life. While Ms. Yates was tempted to take Mr. Hoffman back, she ultimately decided against it, explaining: "Why don't you call me after another six months of therapy and we'll see where we both stand." Ms. Yates has since taken a break from dating to study for the bar exam. After she passes, she intends to take a job as an environmental lawyer and leave the subject of divorce behind her, hopefully, once and for all.

ARE YOU OR YOUR PARTNER SUFFERING FROM EXUS CANNOTGETOVERUS? IF YOU EXHIBIT ELEVEN OR MORE OF THE FOLLOWING SYMTOMS, CONSIDER YOURSELF *GUILTY* AS CHARGED:

1. Retain keepsakes from past relationships, such as letters, photos, emails, and cheesy mix-tapes.

2. Chose lovers who resemble an ex.

3. Change your voice into mellifluous sing-songy pattern when speaking to ex.

4. Find excuses to be in the same place as an ex and frequent former favorite restaurants, bars, and clubs in the hopes ex will be there.

5. Maintain social circles with ex that facilitate continuing contact, which may include relationships with his/her friends and family.

6. Compare all relationships to the one with the ex.

7. Mistakenly call present partner by ex's name on more than one occasion (one will suffice if during a sexual encounter).

8. Still perform favors that ring of a boyfriend/girlfriend quality (i.e., helping him/her move or picking up at airport).

9. Take a peculiar interest in the ex's dating habits.

10. Often bring up the ex with current partner (aka everything reminds him/her of the ex).

11. Use online tools to research the whereabouts of the ex, whether or not there is contact.

12. Make current girlfriend/boyfriend feel like s/he is being unreasonable for suspecting deeper feelings, even where partner maintains a degree of secrecy and/or privacy regarding communication with the ex.

13. Level-headed attempts by partner to discuss ex lead to explosive confrontations, as well as defensive and deflective modes of argument and debate: (a) "Liar lawyer," for example, in which trick questions and deductive reasoning are employed at a feverish pace; (b) "Countertransference," in which the DUPE is accused of *projecting* emotional insecurities; and (c) "Genderflecting," in which the DUPE's accusations are dovetailed by suggesting his/her lack of knowledge/understanding of the psychic mechanisms of the opposite sex.

14. Quickly defend not only his/her platonic intentions, but the ex's as well.

15. Unable to sustain new relationships beyond the first throes of romance, since nobody else compares.

16. Exaggerate the intelligence, beauty, talent, or objective accomplishments of the ex.

17. Romanticize/forget problems/conflicts with the ex.

18. Talk about "fate," and believe that certain people "are meant to be together," suggesting a lingering hope that someday the ex will return; tend to talk about how the future is "a mystery," rather than the result of concrete volition.

19. Do not notice when boundaries are being crossed with regard to the ex.

20. Downplay the degree or intensity of his/her current relationship to the ex or neglect to mention it at all.

DSI MOST WANTED FUGITIVE

WANTED FOR:

INTENTIONAL SEDUCTION THROUGH SACCHARINE PROMISES OF ETERNAL LOVE IN FOREIGN ROMANCE LANGUAGE; DISAPPEARINNG BOTH EMOTIONALLY AND PHYSI-CALLY; BEING ALOOF, DISTANT, AND IMPOSSIBLE TO REACH VIA ORDINARY MODES OF COMMUNICATION

Prescott Horton Sutherland

Aliases: Thurston Howell, Presco the Magician, Horton Gives a Hoot, the Spanish Inquisitor

DESCRIPTION

Date of Birth: 1975

Place of Birth: Newport, RI

Height: 5' 9"

Weight: Approximately 170

Build: Average

Hair: Blonde

Eyes: Blue

Complexion: Light

Sex: Male

Nationality: American

Occupation: Semiprofessional yachtsman

Remarks: Mr. Sutherland is one of DSI's growing number of Most Wanted Fugitives who is also a member of the Social Register. His inclusion on our list forced his family to set up an offshore trust account in the Cayman Islands. Mr. Sutherland considers himself a seaman and, as such, spends considerable time tending to his large vessel in such regions as Chile, Ecuador, and Peru. An avowed romantic, Mr. Sutherland is apt to profess his unfettered adoration for young women of Latin descent in Spanish and then vanish with a teary *adios* some weeks later, pining in English, "The sea is my only mistress." He is currently being hunted by a guerilla army of Costa Rican dissidents for [roughly translated] "Stealing our sisters' souls through a ravaged opening."

Scars and Marks: Typically wears an admiral's uniform, which he purchased at a Sotheby's auction for Gilbert & Sullivan memorabilia; wears a crest ring on his left pinkie; speaks with a distinct Locust Valley Lockjaw accent

CAUTION

MR. SUTHERLAND IS WANTED IN THE AMERICAN TERRITORY OF PUERTO RICO AND VARIOUS SPANISH-SPEAKING PORTS OF CALL THROUGHOUT THE SOUTHERN HEMISPHERE. HIS CRIMINAL USE OF ROMANTIC PERSUASION AND PROMISES OF ETERNAL DEVOTION SUGGEST THAT HE SUFFERS FROM PATHOLOGIC NARCISSISM UNDERSCORED BY TOTAL EMOTIONAL VACANCY.

THIS INDIVIDUAL IS CONSIDERED A MAJOR ROMANTIC THREAT.

A PRIVATE BOUNTY OF 1,000,000 PESOS HAS BEEN OFFERED FOR THE PROFFER OF MR. SUTHERLAND BY AN ANGRY BAND OF SOUTH AMERICAN QUASIMILITANTS.

TEN:

GUESS WHO'S NOT COMING TO DINNER

THE CASE OF THE DISAPPEARING BOYFRIENDS

MISSING BOYFRIENDS: DO YOU KNOW WHERE YOUR MAN IS?

In the post–dial-up world, life is complicated: we move at fiber-optic pace. In our haste, we often misplace things. Items get lost in the shuffle, disappearing before our very eyes, never to be seen again. But we don't expect that to happen to the people we love, do we? Think again. More than 100,000 boyfriends go missing each year in the United States alone (international figures are obscured by European haggling over the definition of "boyfriend"), leaving those behind distraught, confused, and alone. Short of a leash, there is not much to be done about this growing phenomenon. That is, unless you enlist the services of the Missing Boyfriends Unit (MBU).

THE MISSING BOYFRIENDS UNIT

DSI received so many "missing boyfriend" calls in recent years that we decided to establish a special unit dedicated to tracking misplaced boyfriends, at last bringing closure to these perplexing, unsolved mysteries. This special group is known as the Missing Boyfriends Unit. In the following pages, we dig back into the MBU files to present three examples of disappearing boyfriends. As these cases illustrate, boyfriends can go missing in any number of ways. But fear not, for the MBU always gets its man, even if it means tracking him to Timbuktu. We may not be able to force him to date you again, but MBU will seek, find, and force the errant lover to confess to the circumstances that led to his disappearance.

GENERAL DISORDER INFORMATION

Missing boyfriends come in all shapes and sizes. Some go missing physically, while others emotionally vacate—still there in form, but gone in essence. While each missing boyfriend is unique, DSI has identified several general personality profiles that characterize this disorder.

Don Juan Syndrome

This syndrome is marked by a penchant to woo a woman until she falls in love and then break up. Those afflicted tend to engage in theatrical displays of affection; exhibit an unusual degree of enthusiasm for talking about feelings of love and desire for a partner; have a knack for orchestrating the perfect moment with regard to romantic setting, partner-centric lovemaking, and pronouncements of ardor likely to induce a woman to fall head over heels. However, he displays an immediate waning of interest when the woman concedes she is in love and/or talks about domestic matters; has a history of passionate minirelationships lasting around six months or less; and reveals a disdain for anything routine or pragmatic, like household chores.

James Dean Syndrome

A person displaying this disorder exhibits a rebellious streak to strike out on one's own and a concomitant panic of being hemmed in by social/legal obligations. Those afflicted tend to avoid signing leases or buying furniture/real estate; snub planning trips in advance; work in freelance/temp positions rather than 9-to-5 jobs; fail to RSVP for close family weddings; and turn down accidental promotions to management. They consider house plants a major responsibility; prefer cell phones to land lines; think the need for health insurance doesn't pertain to them; use *middle-class* as a pejorative adjective; and have more than a dozen different addresses in a typical two-year span.

Don Quixote Syndrome

This personality is evidenced by delusional fantasies of grandeur unsupported by pragmatic efforts, which leads the perpetrator to break up relationships to pursue "dreams." Those afflicted tend to play in rock bands long into their sixties; own more than one vintage car/Harley that isn't operational; think their blog sites will revolutionize mainstream politics; and presume people who offer them regular jobs are trying to undermine their dreams. They tend to overuse words like *visionary, guru,* and *genius;* feel misunderstood and underappreciated; and say things like, "all it takes is one big break" with reference to absence of identifiable achievements.

Robin Hood Syndrome

A passion to change the world through itinerant grassroots activism causes sufferers of this syndrome to leave long-term partners for a "higher cause." Those afflicted tend to spend extended periods of time in third-world countries; get a funny glow when they discuss severe gastrointestinal ailments acquired while teaching natives how to farm more efficiently; and lament how they would "never bring a child into this polluted, overpopulated world". You'll find that they re-use plastic utensils;

consider gourmet restaurants and vacation resorts a symptom of moral degeneracy; and ascribe more importance to social reform than personal relationships.

John Cheever Syndrome

Long periods of depression, reclusion, or rootless wandering; chemical addiction; and sporadic self-punitive creative expression are hallmarks of this disorder. Those afflicted tend to spend protracted lengths of time without desire for social contact; view the people who love them with contempt; and respond to threatening requests for interaction with remarks like "leave me the f—k alone," and "you're better off without me." They often fail to exercise proper regard for hygiene; refuse to consider mood-elevating medication; believe love, relationships, and all other pursuits are vainglorious exercises of human frailty doomed to failure; and suffer self-loathing for occasionally indulging feelings of love.

MBU FILE ONE: THE GHOST MAN

The Dupe: Patty Caldwell
Age: 25
Location: Phoenix, AZ
Occupation: Kindergarten teacher
Hair: Blonde
Eyes: Green
Height: 5'6"
Weight: 140

Psychographic Thumbnail

Ms. Caldwell is an eternal optimist and do-gooder whose attraction to teaching grew out of a desire to help "shape the minds that will shape the world." A positive thinker prone to describe a near-empty glass as half-full, she often dates men with strains of James Dean and John Cheever

Syndromes, whom she believes she can "rescue." In her past relationships, she has played nurse, social worker, muse, cheerleader, and mother, largely to her own detriment. She has rarely found true fulfillment in these relationships, though caring for another person does meet certain selfish needs to fix and control. More often than not, however, she ends up in relationships that self-destruct, faulting herself for failing to save a romantic partner from the bleakness of living without her. Despite a dim awareness of this instinct, DSI has noticed a pattern that seems almost irreversible, and the case at hand certainly fits the profile of her past history.

The Missing Boyfriend: Aaron Miller
Age: 38
Location: Phoenix, AZ
Occupation: Grad student
Hair: Brown
Eyes: Brown
Height: 5'10"
Weight: 170

Psychographic Thumbnail

Like Ms. Caldwell, Mr. Miller has dreams of enlightening others, in his case with his theories of the world. His course of graduate study in political philosophy grew out of his anger at the mediocrity of mainstream, structured learning, which seeks to reproduce itself rather than embrace iconoclastic thinking, such as his own. He has never been able to fit into the regular working world, and has spent a good deal of time working on his doctorate at various graduate schools. While some, such as his estranged parents, perceive this as an inability to focus or commit (requiring heavy medication), Mr. Miller denounces such opinions as provincial, defending his choices as those of an independent mind yet to find a conduit for meaningful expression. Because of his itinerant lifestyle, most of his past relationships have been borne of convenience.

And none were committed, owing to Mr. Miller's inability to predict when his higher intellectual calling would compel him to leave. His mobility has provided the ultimate escape from long-term intimacy. Mr. Miller does not form deep attachments to his romantic partners and has no concept of how his decision to take off impacts those he leaves behind.

Last Seen

November 12, 2004, exiting the Sandalwood apartment complex in Phoenix, Arizona, at approximately 10:03 A.M.

Circumstances of Disappearance

Based on information compiled from eyewitnesses and field agents, the couple spent the night of November 11, 2004, together after a date that included Cantonese take-out, a documentary film based on the life of Camus borrowed from the University library, a visit to Jamba Juice, and a sexual encounter, which Ms. Caldwell described as "unremarkable." Following a brief morning embrace, Mr. Miller was seen entering his tan 1989 Buick Skylark sedan (California license plate GYX 198), with the ostensible intent to return the film and "meet up sometime later for dinner." Ms. Caldwell did not hear from Mr. Miller for the next three days, despite leaving him two voicemails and one email marked "urgent." She consequently stopped by the graduate dorm and found his room unlocked with all of his personal belongings removed. Ms. Caldwell then knocked on the door of a twenty-four-year-old Caucasian male next door and inquired if he'd seen her missing boyfriend. "Oh Miller? Yeah, he said he was like going to Oregon or Mexico or something to study. He gave me this cactus plant. You want it?" Ms. Caldwell tearfully accepted the plant, which she had given him for his last birthday, figuring even he could manage the watering commitment.

RELATIONSHIP RECONNAISSANCE

Mr. Miller and Ms. Caldwell met on a warm evening in the fall of 2003 at the graduate library of University of Arizona after a screening of the movie *Eraserhead*. A San Francisco native who enrolled in a Ph.D. program at UC Santa Cruz, Mr. Miller had come to the university to do research for his dissertation on tribal governments in early Indian settlements. A keen interest in alternative cinema led him to attend the screening. Ms. Caldwell had seen a flyer for the event at a local coffee shop and decided she could stand a break from six-year-olds. After exchanging a couple of smiles during the movie, Ms. Caldwell approached Mr. Miller during the wine and cheese reception. After telling Mr. Miller she was an early childhood teacher at a progressive Montessori, Mr. Miller expressed his approval, and they spoke animatedly about the stunting of the creative imagination through traditional public education. Passionate about her career, Ms. Caldwell was immediately taken by Mr. Miller's atypical interest in her work and his thoughtful denunciation of "cookie-cutter schooling." At the end of the evening, when Mr. Miller failed to ask Ms. Caldwell for her phone number, she took the initiative and invited him over for dinner the next night.

Dinner was lovely and the conversation lively, but Ms. Caldwell noticed a certain peripatetic quality to Mr. Miller's manner. While he spoke with great enthusiasm about tribal government hierarchies, his eyes did not light up nearly as much when they spoke of more personal matters, such as their childhoods, families, and friends. Nonetheless, they discovered a mutual interest in hiking and camping, and made plans to explore the desert landscape together.

Mr. Miller proved to be an athletic, though not a particularly intimate lover, and the two started spending most nights together at her apartment, enjoying an active sex life. When Ms. Caldwell finally asked to see his dorm room in the hopes of gleaning more information about his background, she was taken aback that he did not have a single photo or keepsake. When she tried to press him on whether he was close with his parents or homesick for old friends, he grew remote and laconic, claiming that he was trying to live simply.

For the next six months of the relationship, Mr. Miller was a perfect partner. The only time she saw glimpses of that distant quality she'd apprehended earlier was when the subject turned to family. Ms. Caldwell told Mr. Miller that she felt his pain, and that she didn't want to pressure him to talk about whatever was bothering him until he was ready, but that she would love him unconditionally. Mr. Miller changed the subject to his travels, which were very extensive, different from anyone Ms. Caldwell had met before.

On weekends, the couple went on long hikes, making love under the stars wherever they happened to wind up at day's end. Ms. Caldwell found Mr. Miller's spontaneity, virility, and rugged facility for building a fire and pitching a tent intoxicating. So she asked him to move in with her, inducing that vacant look again. Only this time it didn't go away.

Over the next few weeks, Mr. Miller spent less time with Ms. Caldwell, ostensibly working around the clock on his dissertation. On the night before his ultimate disappearance, the couple had gotten into a discussion regarding Thanksgiving plans. Ms. Caldwell had invited him to spend the weekend with her family, saying: "I know you aren't close to your family. So I want you to think of my family as your own. They will welcome you with open arms and make you see that a family can be a place of love and nurturing, not pain." Mr. Miller nodded absently, and the two made love. Ms. Caldwell figured he needed to let the information process.

The next morning was the last she ever saw Mr. Miller. When she did not hear from him for three days, and found his dorm room cleared out, Ms. Caldwell filed a Missing Boyfriend Report. Ms. Caldwell still believes she can help Mr. Miller overcome whatever childhood trauma he suffered and teach him the "true meaning of family."

INVESTIGATION AND ASSESSMENT

Physical Evidence

An investigation into Mr. Miller's university records show that he had notified the housing office of his intent to leave six weeks prior to his disappearance, reporting: "completed all archival research at the university and Pueblo Museum as planned." He did not specify which school he would be attending next, listing a post office box in San Rafael, California, as his forwarding address. He had returned his dorm key before he went over to Ms. Caldwell's apartment for the last time. A sweep of his room, including dust and fingerprint analysis, verified that Mr. Miller never returned to his room after kissing Ms. Caldwell goodbye.

A full search of the room yielded the following additional findings:

→ Hair samples that matched Mr. Miller's DNA type showed that he had dyed his hair darker approximately eight months earlier.

→ Internet footprints showed Google searches pertaining to tribal government and free university housing in both Eugene, Oregon, and San Miguel de Allende, Mexico.

→ A sealed container of Wellbutrin was retrieved from the garbage (a common treatment for clinical depression).

→ A dozen unopened letters were found in the garbage, from Dr. and Mrs. Miller of Larkspur, California (a suburb of San Francisco).

MBU LOCATOR REPORT

Based on the physical evidence and our own MBU network of field agents affiliates, we were able to deduce that Mr. Miller headed due south into Mexico. Passport controls confirmed this suspicion, but it was a subsequent MBU report that sealed our investigation. On his way south, Mr. Miller had wooed and won over a librarian in San Diego. He had disappeared from her clutches as well, but not before revealing to her his dream of studying the native peoples of Todos Santos in the Baja California peninsula.

RECOVERED BOYFRIEND TESTIMONY

Mr. Miller was apprehended by MBU and brought in for questioning, where it was revealed that he had indeed "disappeared" from Arizona because of emotional pressures brought on by his relationship with Ms. Caldwell. Upon seeing Mr. Miller, Ms. Caldwell immediately began crying and told him she could help him "heal if only given half a chance."

"You did nothing wrong," Mr. Miller replied, a distant look clouding his eyes. "That's not who I am. I don't want a family. Not yours. Not mine. You're a wonderful woman and deserve all the happiness in the world. But I don't have it in me to offer."

When she asked why he hadn't at least said goodbye, he said, "It's easier this way." Mr. Miller and Ms. Caldwell left the way they came, separately.

DSI FINDING

In this case, a troubled past preempted a fulfilling future. Specifically, Mr. Miller lacks the ability to stay rooted, either physically or emotionally. This brand of inability to commit is often disguised by a desire to travel the world and immerse oneself in foreign/unfamiliar cultures. With sufficient dedication and therapy, Mr. Miller may one day prove to be a wonderful, caring partner. But for now, his wounds prevent him from being more than a temporary companion. Ms. Caldwell would be wise to confront her own insecurities, so she can at last find a partner, rather than a project, to share her love. Mr. Miller will likely remain a serial missing boyfriend until he recognizes his own fears of intimacy and considers how his behavior impacts those who care for him.

MBU FILE TWO: THE FADEAWAY

The Dupe: Melissa Wong
Age: 32
Location: New York, NY

Occupation: Publicist
Hair: Brown
Eyes: Brown
Height: 5'7"
Weight: 130

Psychographic Thumbnail

Ms. Wong is, like many New York women in their early thirties, torn between a liberated lifestyle and more "traditional" desires to settle down and start a family. She is successful and independent, and has spent most of her post-collegiate life building a career and dating in serial fashion. She has had plenty of fun along the way, but is now beginning to worry about finding a long-term partner. Not prone to follow *The Rules*, she has often rushed into sexual situations, without taking the time to develop a foundation of friendship. Her relationships tend to start off with a proverbial bang and then fizzle out just as quickly. Her women friends seem to fall into one of two categories: married with two kids or terminal daters, out there burning up the New York social scene. She is somewhere in the middle, but finds it difficult to meet like-minded men who want to have a good time while entertaining longer-range goals of marriage and children.

The Missing Boyfriend: Jason Gastonbury
Age: 35
Location: New York, NY
Occupation: Banker
Hair: Brown
Eyes: Hazel
Height: 6'1"
Weight: 180

Psychographic Thumbnail

Like many men in New York City, Jason Gastonbury is a "successful" serial dater. This has less to do with his charms or looks, although he has both in ample measure, and more to do with the mechanics of urban dating. For him, as for many men, the numbers work in his favor. The constant supply of dating prospects has led him to take things for granted to a certain extent. When the moment is right, he figures he will find himself a serious partner. Until then, he plans to enjoy life to the fullest, which means keeping it light. Mr. Gastonbury does not consider himself mean or malicious. He gives generously to children's charities, participates in Breast Cancer Awareness and AIDS walkathons, and calls his mother every other Sunday like clockwork. Nonetheless, his dating record shows a history of negligence when it comes to matters of the heart. At the age of thirty-five, Mr. Gastonbury is settled in his career, makes a good living, and affords a comfortable lifestyle. He takes dates to the finest restaurants and regularly woos women with fancy vacations to exotic locales. He has never been married, though he once came close. He ended the relationship, explaining he was "not yet ready to settle down." While this seemed to him an honest assessment, it is borne more out of a larger fear of commitment than out of any deep level of self-awareness.

Last Seen

Exiting the restaurant/bar Serafina, in lower Manhattan, around 3:00 A.M. hours, on Thursday, February 8, 2005. He was in the company of small, mixed-gender group. Ms. Wong was not among this group.

Last Known Contact

Last known physical interaction occurred one night prior to the aforementioned sighting. Subsequent contact with Ms. Wong was limited to scattered text messages and emails, the last of which was received on February 28, 2005.

Circumstances of Disappearance

The evening before physical disappearance, Ms. Wong had canceled dinner reservations and treated Mr. Gastonbury to an elaborate home-cooked, candlelit meal of oysters Rockefeller, pan-seared Atlantic swordfish, and truffle polenta. After lighting the bananas flambé, she handed Mr. Gastonbury a key to her apartment, asking him for one in return, so they could "surprise each other" on late work nights. Mr. Gastonbury thanked Ms. Wong for the key and promised to make one to his apartment. He smiled graciously saying "he would love nothing more than to discover her in his bed," but left immediately after dinner (accidentally leaving the key behind) claiming a Saturday morning breakfast meeting downtown. Later that day, he left Ms. Wong a text message indicating that he had to cancel their regular Saturday night date to attend a "business dinner." The MBU sighting would seem to contradict this statement. As he exited Serafina, he was seen entering a cab with two of the five members of the group (one female, one male). While MBU was unable to track his whereabouts thereafter (due to crosstown traffic and a stalled bus), voice recordings from the last known locale suggest they were going to another club. Since said time, anonymous tips have suggested that Mr. Gastonbury has been spotted at various exclusive restaurants and clubs in downtown, New York City as well as in East Hampton, NY, and the Delano Hotel in Miami South Beach.

RELATIONSHIP RECONNAISSANCE

Mr. Gastonbury and Ms. Wong met in the summer of 2004 at a dinner party hosted by a mutual acquaintance in New York City. It was unusual that they both happened to be in the city that weekend (as they each had summer shares in the Hamptons). For Mr. Gastonbury, the chance meeting seemed like a stroke of fate, one which he felt compelled to act upon. For her part, Ms. Wong found Mr. Gastonbury attractive, but made it a policy never to date investment bankers, having previously found them egocentric and immature. Mr. Gastonbury was, nonetheless, up for the chase. After securing Ms. Wong's email from the party's host ("she thinks you're cute, but you have to show her you really care," said the hostess), he began a focused campaign of courtship. His emails were witty and charming, not to mention emotionally forthcoming about to his intent to make her "fall for" him, suggesting more than a desire for a brief sexual liaison. Ms. Wong at last agreed to meet him for a dinner date.

While she was skeptical from the get-go, she soon warmed to his demonstrable show of affection, and his seduction proved successful. This owed in part to Ms. Wong's desire to find a relationship. At thirty-two, her parents and family often joked about her single status. Every wedding she got invited to seemed to hammer home this point. After she turned thirty, she promised herself to start making more informed choices in men, and to look for qualities she desired in a long-term mate. Her therapist told her relationships were about compromises, and if Mr. Gastonbury was not perfect, he appeared extremely eager to please her and possessed an unusual ability to balance a successful career with a healthy enjoyment of life. Ms. Wong soon found herself dating Mr. Gastonbury, and before she knew it, she had a boyfriend. This made her happy, and she was able to commit herself fully to the relationship, eschewing her former feelings of uncertainty.

The two fell into a semiserious relationship, spending weekends together, and getting to the point where they kept clothes and toothbrushes at each other's apartments. For Ms. Wong, this was a significant step. All of her recent romantic efforts had either ended on the first date or resulted in casual, short-lived flings. Mr. Gastonbury, for his part, was awfully good at playing the role of boyfriend, and he too enjoyed the pleasures and convenience of regular companionship.

At the six-month mark of the relationship, Ms. Wong surprised Mr. Gastonbury by planning a romantic weekend getaway at a New England Inn, which appeared to go off very pleasantly. It was after this weekend, however, that Mr. Gastonbury began to complain that he was busy at work, and the amount of time they spent together subsequently diminished. Ms. Wong tried to be understanding, telling Mr. Gastonbury that they did not always have to go out to gourmet restaurants or hip clubs, and that she would be delighted to spend more time "at home together."

Mr. Gastonbury replied that a lovely lady like Ms. Wong deserved royal treatment, and promised to have more time for her after he finished up a top priority project at the firm's San Francisco office, which required long hours and frequent weekends of work. Mr. Gastonbury did not indicate any unhappiness with the relationship. He simply explained that this was an unforeseeable job requirement.

Instead of spending two or three nights a week together, they were soon spending no more than one. On the eve of the disappearance, Ms. Wong decided to show Mr. Gastonbury that she was perfectly content to cook for him and spend quiet evenings "at home," and had thus given him her apartment key so he could come over whenever he wanted. She has not seen him or spoken with him since, their limited exchanges restricted to text messages and email.

INVESTIGATION AND ASSESSMENT

Physical Evidence

The MBU analyzed the series of text messages and emails that Mr. Gastonbury sent during the period of "slow fade-out." By electronically tracking the points of origin of these messages, it was determined that most were sent from various points within the metropolitan New York area, from locations in Tribeca and Soho. Two of the messages were sent from points outside the New York City area: one from Miami South Beach and the other from Coconut Grove, Florida. None were traced to the San Francisco area, where Mr. Gastonbury was purported to be stationed during this time frame.

A linguistic assessment of emails and text messages sent during the "fade-out" period were consistent with passive-aggression/commitment phobia: "Sorry dear, must cancel on account of pressing deadline (yuck!)"; "Apologies again, let's do it another time!"; and "Can't make it back this weekend, hope you're having a better time than I am!!"

Other physical evidence uncovered by the MBU team included the following:

→ A thorough search of all airline databases confirmed that Mr. Gastonbury had never made any trips to the San Francisco area, but did reveal two weekend flights for two to Miami.

→ Bouncers at club B.E.D. in both New York and South Beach reported having seen the man in the photo (example, Mr. Gastonbury) with a very tall African-American woman who "looks like a Victoria's Secret model."

→ The receptionist at Mr. Gastonbury's Wall Street firm, who has asked to remain anonymous, reported that Mr. Gastonbury was not assigned to any special projects at satellite offices during this time and was advised that if Ms. Wong called, she was to say: "I'm sorry, but Mr. Gastonbury is out of the office this week."

→ Mr. Gastonbury's concierge, who prefers to remain anonymous, reported arranging dinner reservations for two several times during the "fade-out" period, and that Mr. Gastonbury had been accompanied by a very tall African-American woman who "looks like a Victoria's Secret model."

MBU LOCATOR REPORT

Using dedicated DSI satellites triangulated to Mr. Gastonbury's Blackberry, the MBU was able to locate Mr. Gastonbury in his Gramercy Park condominium, where he was apprehended and brought in for questioning. As suspected, he was "lost" amid the island of Manhattan, hiding in plain sight. His business trip was simply a ruse designed to facilitate his "fade-away" plan, as were the emails and text messages he sent following his disappearance. During booking, Mr. Gastonbury voluntarily admitted that he was "in love with falling in love" and had engaged in six-month romances at least a dozen times. Based on his statement against interest, Mr. Gastonbury has been officially flagged by DSI as a repeat offender.

RECOVERED BOYFRIEND TESTIMONY

Upon seeing Ms. Wong in the interrogation room, Mr. Gastonbury made a feeble attempt to flee from custody, but found himself up against a wall. He smiled at her sheepishly and commented that she was looking "lovely as always." Given his past history, the MBU was anxious to capture his testimony, as he was thought to be representative of a larger breed of single urban men.

When she asked him to explain his conduct, Mr. Gastonbury avoided making eye contact with Ms. Wong and told the MBU agent: "I honestly don't think I did anything wrong. I took her to great restaurants and on lovely vacations, no expense spared. We had a wonderful, memorable time together. I never said I was looking for marriage, only love. And when I realized she had gotten the wrong idea in her head about where our relationship was headed, I did the right thing and ended it."

Ms. Wong interrupted: "Why didn't you come right out and tell me? Why did you drag it out like that? Why didn't you have the decency to tell me in person how you felt?"

Mr. Gastonbury replied to the MBU agent: "We dated, it didn't work out, and I let her know I was no longer interested, in so many words. I tried to be honest, but the fade-away was a way of letting her down easy. It's not easy to end something with someone, and she's a great girl. She's just not for me."

Mr. Gastonbury was silent. Then he forced himself to look at Ms. Wong directly. "I didn't want to see the hurt and disappointment in your eyes. I just wanted to remember the way you used to gaze at me when we first fell in love."

When asked whether he felt any obligation to apologize to Ms. Wong, or any desire to let her know the truth, he added that, "All is fair in dating, though I do hope she is doing well. She deserves a nice guy. Maybe that is not me."

DSI FINDING

A clear-cut case of Don Juan Syndrome, Mr. Gastonbury is hardly unique in the metropolitan dating world. In fact, Mr. Gastonbury's "fade-away" is the most common form of disappearing boyfriend at MBU. At its most basic level, men afflicted with some form of this syndrome are addicted to the chase and first flourish of romance, losing interest when the relationship becomes more settled and domestic. Their desire to be desired and loved in the moment without complications makes breaking up in person that much more difficult. And so they tend to "fade away," rather than actually end things, hoping to leave things on a positive note. Our societal reliance on electronic forms of communication makes the "fade-out" that much easier, as it is easy to be in touch without putting anything at stake. While communicating electronically has the positive effect of allowing people to get to know each other better in a nonsexual setting, especially when hectic work schedules make physical presence untenable, the impersonal nature of the medium makes it easier for us to devalue the flesh-and-blood person who resides at the other end of the cybersphere. The compounded online opportunities for pursuing new relationships without sacrificing too much time or risk has also contributed to the commoditization of dating into a virtual marketplace where ready supply has cheapened demand. Men like Mr. Gastonbury, who can continue to avoid intimacy without losing out on the benefits of romance, companionship, and sex, have yielded the maximum rewards. Single women, like Ms. Wong, for whom fertility creates a more finite timeline, have, on the contrary, suffered. While the Internet and its offshoots make it easier to meet people, they have also served to devalue relationships. All too often people who date treat each other like virtual commodities, not human beings. As Mr. Gastonbury's behavior indicates, it is often an "every man for himself" attitude that pervades today's urban dating arena.

MBU FILE THREE: THERE IN BODY, NOT IN HEART

The Dupe: Amanda Parsons
Age: 30
Location: Stamford, CT
Occupation: Pastry chef
Hair: Blonde
Eyes: Brown
Height: 5'2"
Weight: 125

Psychographic Thumbnail

A Florida native, Ms. Parsons relocated to Stamford, Connecticut, following an amicable divorce from her college-football-playing boyfriend. While the two agreed it was a starter marriage, the dissolution of the relationship was difficult, since the couple had been together for many years despite a fundamental lack of passion or common interests. It also inspired her to make some positive changes in her life. She moved from the state where she'd grown up and purchased a small bakery she'd found advertised in the *Miami Herald* located in downtown Stamford, a suburb of New York City. She has succeeded in building a new life for herself, and has found an ample community of friends. While she has enjoyed being on her own, she realizes she is now ready to delve into a more serious relationship, hopefully including marriage and children. But given the long, unusual hours she works in the bakery (from 4:00 A.M. to 3:00 P.M. daily), she has found it difficult to meet potential partners. She has therefore opened herself up to more innovative dating methods, including speed dating and online dating services.

The Missing Boyfriend: Robert Landau
Age: 34
Location: Greenwich, CT
Occupation: Architect

Hair: Brown
Eyes: Green
Height: 6'
Weight: 165

Psychographic Thumbnail

Mr. Landau is a workaholic bachelor who has lived in Greenwich, Connecticut, all his life. As the founder of one of the region's top architectural design firms, his career takes precedence, leaving him little time to date. He also has many outside interests, including chamber music and tennis. Though he says he is looking forward to getting married and starting a family, whenever he gets close to a potential partner, his conviction crumbles as to whether she is "the one," and the relationship grinds to a halt. He then refocuses his attention on his business without giving further thought to the matter. He has never been married, and has twice called off engagements, deciding the women did not possess some unidentifiable quality he required in a life partner. Mr. Landau's parents divorced when he was thirteen. His father's announcement that he was leaving "to find himself" came as a complete shock to both his wife and son. He left them comfortably situated financially, but has had no further contact with either of them. Mr. Landau's mother, a social worker, never dated again and greeted every question by her son about why his father left with the phrase: "He will always love you. I'm sorry."

Last Seen

While Mr. Landau has not disappeared physically, he has been emotionally absent for some time. According to Ms. Parson's testimony and MBU psychographic profiling, it has been determined that he "checked out" on April 7, 2005, after he and Ms. Parsons celebrated eight months of dating.

Circumstances of Disappearance

To commemorate eight months of dating (eight is Ms. Parsons' "lucky number," and her bakery is named "Eight Ate"), Mr. Landau rented a beachside cabin in Key West for a weekend of fun, frolicking, and fishing. Things seemed to be going well until the final night when, following a dinner, Mr. Landau complained of indigestion. From that moment forward, according to Ms. Parsons, "it was like he was in a waking coma."

RELATIONSHIP RECONNAISSANCE

Mr. Landau and Ms. Parsons met through one of the nation's largest online dating services, geared toward helping people find partners who share common interests, values, and goals. After being notified by the service that Mr. Landau was her closest match, Ms. Parsons bucked convention and made the first move, sending Mr. Landau a flirty note that made reference to his work and her love of "big buildings." Mr. Landau was both amused and impressed, and the two began a long email correspondence, discovering they shared a similar work ethic along with a passion for chamber music and tennis. When they finally coordinated their busy schedules to meet for dinner, they found they had strong physical chemistry, too. After passing the "in person test," they soon embarked on a romantic affair. Both were very happy with the situation from the onset, and the relationship had all the hallmarks of a mature, serious connection, including open lines of communication and respect for one another's entrepreneurial bent and need for alone time.

Both were also open about their histories. While Ms. Parsons was concerned her divorce might be a negative, Mr. Landau told her that he felt it gave her more experience and insight into herself, and thus considered it "a positive." Mr. Landau, in turn, talked about the pain of his father's unexpected departure and how it made him leery of the prospect of marriage. This was why he thought it so crucial to take the time and find the "perfect mate," to ensure that his marital vows would last. Given her own experience, Ms. Parsons was uniquely sympathetic to Mr. Landau's motivation to "get it right the first time." Upon hearing that he had broken up two ostensibly happy engagements, however, she grew concerned that his desire might be partially rooted in phobia and unresolved trauma. She therefore suggested he consider professional therapy, which she herself had sought following her own divorce. Mr. Landau said he might consider it, but never followed through.

Despite these potential pitfalls, the relationship progressed. Both Mr. Landau and Ms. Parsons were often busy with work, but they worked around their various schedules to spend quality time together. Ms. Parsons observed that she was more "flexible" in this regard than Mr. Landau, often meeting him for dinner after 9:00 P.M. despite having to wake up at 3:00 A.M. She also noticed that there were times when he seemed overly preoccupied with a project, causing him to talk about work issues late into the night without regard for her schedule or how her own business was faring.

When Ms. Parsons confronted Mr. Landau about the dynamic, he apologized sincerely and promised to do better. He thereupon decided to take her away for a long romantic weekend where they could get away from the ordinary pressures of everyday life. He concluded by saying "I love you" for the first time, a sentiment Ms. Parsons was delighted to echo. The first three days and nights of their tropical getaway were idyllic. They played tennis, spent long afternoons fishing, cooked side by side, and made love to chamber music in the salty sea air. When, on their final night together, Mr. Landau suddenly went "missing in action," Ms. Parsons grew worried.

Now a full month after their return, the couple continues to spend most nights together. But Mr. Landau has remained "absent" and emotionally disengaged. When Ms. Parsons has tried to discuss her concerns, he tells her "I love you" with vacant eyes and falls silent, claiming he is simply trying to be more sensitive by not bringing work home. Each time Ms. Parsons raises the issue, he retreats even further. Ms. Parsons has turned to MBU as a last resort, hoping to turn things around before it's too late.

INVESTIGATION AND ASSESSMENT

Psychological Evidence

The case before us presents a more complex set of issues than its predecessors, as Mr. Landau appears to be in thrall to his own unconscious motives. Not falling under any of the standard profiles of a Missing Boyfriend, the MBU must focus its examination not merely on the physical evidence, but on the underlying emotional factors at play.

In this case, the physical evidence suggests that Mr. Landau remains committed to the relationship:

→ Mr. Landau has not fled the relationship or tried to push Ms. Parsons away.

→ MBU tracking units have discovered the presence of Ms. Parson's personal effects throughout Mr. Landau's living space.

→ MBU field agents have spotted Mr. Landau surveying various high-end jewelry stores in search of engagement rings.

→ Mr. Landau has made no effort to disguise what he admits are emotional hurdles.

The psychological evidence, however, tells a different story:

→ Despite his awareness, Mr. Landau has made no efforts to explore these issues with a therapist.

→ He is often cold and distant to Ms. Parsons, especially when she tries to discuss his apparent "disconnect."

→ Email traces reveal that Mr. Landau located and wrote to his estranged father several times in recent months seeking answers and prospective resolution, even offering forgiveness, but his father failed to reply. [Mr. Landau's emails were return receipted, indicating that the emails were successfully delivered and read.]

MBU LOCATOR REPORT

The MBU team was dispatched to Mr. Landau's place of employment during the evening of May 7, 2005. Mr. Landau was the only person present in his office at the time. He peacefully turned himself in, fully apprised of the nature of the indictment for his being "emotionally AWOL."

RECOVERED BOYFRIEND TESTIMONY

When questioned, Mr. Landau lapsed into silence, his eyes glazed over in a manner suggesting further retreat. Upon being reminded of the nature of the proceeding, he visibly forced himself to respond to Ms. Parsons' interrogation.

"What made you disappear like that all of a sudden that night?" she asked imploringly.

"I was sad that the weekend was about to end," he said earnestly. "It made me anxious, I guess. I thought about how wonderful it would be to wake up next to you for the rest of our lives, and then it seemed like it was all going to disappear. That's the last thing I remember thinking."

The MBU therapist urged Mr. Landau to continue: "I know it's difficult, but I want you to try and remember the stray thoughts that played in the back of your mind over the past month with regard to your feelings for Ms. Parsons."

"Hmm. Well . . . I think that the closer we got as a couple, the more I started wondering if we were going to wind up like my parents. I have no idea what was going through my father's head that day he left. Maybe he turned off, like I sometimes do. Or maybe he suddenly realized that my mother wasn't the right woman for him. And the fact that Ms. Parsons was divorced only added to my fears. In a way, it gave her insight, but in another, it made me concerned she might not know if something was right, since she'd gotten it wrong before."

"But what in particular went through your head in Key West before you hit the final disconnect? Was it something I said or did?" asked Ms. Parsons.

"This is going to be weird, but when my father left us that day, well, he never said goodbye to me. I saw him leaving the house with lots of luggage. When I went downstairs, I saw my mother crying. I'd never seen her like that before. I asked her where my dad went. I guess she didn't want to break it to me just like that or maybe she was hoping he'd change his mind, so she told me he'd gone off on a fishing trip. But then days passed and weeks passed . . . and well, he never came back. And anytime I asked my mom about it, she'd sort of get all stony-eyed and tell me she was sorry and that my father loved me. You know, that day in the cabin, there was this old guy fishing right outside the back window. And for a second I thought, maybe it's my dad. Maybe he tracked me here. And then the next thing I knew I just froze up."

DSI FINDING

The case at hand is one of the few successful MBU missions. Most of the time, the MBU recovery team is tasked with recovering a boyfriend whose very act of fleeing demonstrates he is not a worthy choice. In those situations, our aim is to offer the DUPE one last opportunity to get answers, for her peace of mind. In Mr. Landau's case, however, his strong emotional attachment to Ms. Parsons, his open admission of anxiety, and even his recent efforts to find his father demonstrate a heartfelt desire to confront his past and move forward. Like many people, Mr. Landau's fear of commitment was rooted in unresolved issues that had nothing to do with the person he was dating. It's going to take considerable time, patience, and hard work on both their parts, but in our estimation, this couple has got what it takes to make it.

FOLLOW-UP

A one-year follow-up found Mr. Landau and Ms. Parsons engaged to be married. Mr. Landau is now seeing a therapist on a weekly basis. While he realizes that his questions regarding his father's disappearance may never be answered, he is not going to let that prevent him from having a loving family of his own. He and Ms. Landau are planning to honeymoon in Paris, and to avoid all future fishing excursions pending further notice.

THE GANG OF FOUR

This case presents a rare situation where a group of women who dated the same ARSE banded together to form a posse, and made an arrest en masse. Each of the so-called "Gang of Four" had been spurned by the ARSE, thirty-two-year-old Fredrick Childs, of Cincinnati, Ohio. In two instances, Mr. Childs committed continuous acts of infidelity. In the other two, Mr. Childs was aloof, unresponsive, and intermittently unfaithful. The thread that bound this posse together was the temporal overlap that, remarkably, tied each situation together: at one point Mr. Childs was dating and/or involved with all four woman at the same time.

None of the women knew about the others, and each of the purported "relationships" was bound by a presumption of exclusivity. Each had met Mr. Childs via a dating website, and had been charmed by his profile, handsome photographs, purported desire for "a long-term committed relationship leading to marriage," and witty email banter, in which he specifically derided "game-playing," "cheating," and "dishonesty." None of the women had cause to suspect they were part of a long string of women he had wooed, with no intention but to date for a short period of time. Mr. Childs was what DSI labels "a sport dater," which, while not a disorder, constitutes the actionable tort of "dating misconduct" when evidence shows a willful misrepresentation with intent to seduce marked by reckless disregard for emotional duress.

Mr. Childs defends his actions by contending that he does, in fact, value honesty and fidelity, and hopes to find a marital partner, as claimed. Moreover, he alleges that the women had constructive knowledge (i.e., they "knew or should have known," that his profile was still active while they were dating him). As such, they were negligent for failing to note Mr. Childs' continuing online presence in the dating chat room and his status of "single and looking." Said the ARSE: "They could have tracked my recent online activity. Besides, online dating is not like real dating. Nobody is seriously committed."

The women became apprised of each other's involvement with Mr. Childs from an email sent by Mr. Childs himself. To wit, the ARSE sent an email to one woman, but addressed her by another woman's name. The four women then found each other on the dating service message board. Upon initiating a class action against Mr. Childs, they went back and charted the various points of overlap, gathering factual proof of his fraudulent claims of "honesty" and "fidelity." Mr. Childs' subsequent capture and apprehension demonstrates a brilliant coordination of efforts toward one common end, or ARSE.

One of the women set up a date with Mr. Childs at a well-known restaurant where he had taken all of the women before (it was his trademark date place). The others arranged with the dining establishment (which had long noted Mr. Childs' dating conduct) to go "undercover" as the waitress, the hostess, and the bartender. Soon after the "couple" was seated, his date made a delightfully naughty request, daring Mr. Childs to unzip his fly and avail himself of a rousing game of footsy. Mr. Childs happily complied. At this point, he was confronted by the other three women: each came out, in succession, to dump something on Mr. Childs' lap. The bartender chose red wine; the hostess splattered the ink from her pen; the waitress dropped a plate of spaghetti marinara on his crotch.

When Mr. Childs stood up, his manhood doused in motley sauce, a local newspaper reporter and photographer (arranged by the Gang of Four) snapped photos of his capture and arrest. The event received front-page billing, and the Gang of Four were instantly dubbed the "female four musketeers of dating." The Gang has since turned their escapades into a reality/crime-stopper television show aimed at catching ARSEs like Mr. Childs in action.

DSI wishes to commend these valiant women for their time, dedication, and ingenious resourcefulness, earning them a coveted place in the DSI Hall of Fame.

And for all those ARSEs out there, be forewarned: we'll be watching you.

DSI GLOSSARY OF FORENSIC TERMS

A-BUST—After BreakUp Sex Tryst. Often better than sex during the relationship and frequently mistaken for a sign of lingering romantic chemistry.

ARSE—Anti-Relationship Suspect Examinee. The individual about whom a DUPE has placed a DSI 911 call. ARSES are the main perpetrators of crimes of the heart in the DSI case files and are usually (though not always) male.

BBT—Baby Talk Tendencies. Often uncovered during VPA (Voice Pattern Analysis) of cell-phone calls between a male ARSE and any of his ex-girlfriends; BBT is indicative of a level of emotional involvement between ARSE and Ex that runs counter to any and all assertions of a purely platonic friendship.

BOLT—Body and Oral Language Test. A standard DSI test to interpret body language and subtext.

CAD—Cunnilingus Antagonist Disorder. A form of sexual "ill-cliteracy" in which a male ARSE does not understand, appreciate, or respect the role of clitoral stimulation in stimulating female sexual response, and often expresses aversion to engaging in oral sex. Men with CAD often maintain a double-standard and feel entitled to receive oral stimulation without any obligation to give.

CAT Scan—Cellular Analysis Tapping Scan. A tap placed on some to all of an ARSE's electronic devices, including cell phone and Blackberry, when a reasonable likelihood of dating malfeasance warrants such a privacy intrusion.

CLIT—Clitoral Literacy Impairment Test. An infrared scanning technology used to measure an ARSE's basic understanding of, and appreciation for, female anatomy and sexual pleasuring.

CLOG—Concealed Lack of Orgasmic Gratification. Often referred to as simply "faking it," this complex syndrome involves a general failure to communicate sexual dissatisfaction and a concomitant fear, primarily among DUPEs, to discuss sexual needs and desires.

CoDAC—Co-Dependency Assessment Correlation. A series of tests conducted by DSI to determine one's susceptibility to fall into co-dependent patterns of behavior.

CRAP—Commitment-Repellant Assessment Placement Test. Used to pinpoint the relative degree of an ARSE's inability to commit. Results are based on a variety of oral, behavioral, and psychographic factors, including body language and physical responses to emotional stimuli, leading to a final determination ranging from "not to worry" to "hang in there, baby" to "hide the Häagen Daaz."

Dating DNA. The individual and collective sexual, psychological, and emotional "fingerprints" involving a subject ARSE and DUPE.

DENIAL—Divorce Evaluation Not In A Lifetime Test. Determines the likelihood that a married, cheating ARSE will leave his or her current spouse.

DICK—Determined Inability to Commit Kabash. Where an ARSE's inability to commit threatens the success of a relationship. Left untreated, such inability spells the death knell of the relationship.

DOLT—Degree of Occupational Limitation Test. Used to determine how much a party to a relationship is relying on his or her career to keep emotional attachments and relationships at bay.

Don Juan Syndrome. Marked by a penchant to woo a woman until she falls in love and then break up. Those afflicted tend to engage in theatrical displays of affection, exhibit an unusual degree of enthusiasm for talking about feelings of love and desire for a partner, and have a knack for orchestrating the perfect moment with regard to romantic setting.

Don Quixote Syndrome. Marked by delusional fantasies of grandeur unsupported by pragmatic efforts, which lead them to break up relationship to pursue "their dreams." Those afflicted tend to play in rock bands long into their sixties, own more than one vintage car/Harley that isn't operational, and think their blog sites will revolutionize mainstream politics.

DREAD—Dysfunctional Relationship Evaluation Assessment Database. Often deployed by DSI data miners in conjunction with NERD to assess whether the members of a couple—based on previous dating history and psychographic factors—meet the basic threshold of emotional capacity to engage in a mutually rewarding, long-term relationship.

DSR—Date Scene Reconstruction. A blow-by-blow replay of pivotal encounters throughout the relationship to illuminate romantic obstacles and dating potential in a case at hand.

DUD—Dead Upon Departure. A relationship that was doomed from the get-go based on fundamental absence of compatibility and/or lack of sexual chemistry of either or both of the parties.

DUPE—Desperately Under Pressure to Evaluate. The individual who places initial 911 call to DSI, seeking an investigation into an ARSE. The majority of dating DUPES are female, though there are exceptions this rule.

DWI—Dialing While Intoxicated. Those regrettable phone calls an injured party to a relationship makes when sobriety is lacking.

Ex-Files. DSI's vast database of relationships gone awry and the ARSE's who have knowingly perpetrated crimes of the heart.

Ex-PAT—Ex–Post Assessment Test. A forensic review of magnetic resonance imaging of brain and heart-rate patterns to determine an ARSE's true level of interest in another party with whom he has had previous engagements.

Exus Cannotgetoverus. A dating disorder marked by an overly friendly bond between former romantic partners. The disorder can range from a mild sense of nostalgia for the ex to a debilitating level of obsession, although most cases fall somewhere in between.

FBI—Federal Bureau of Intimacy. DSI's supervising governmental agency.

FIB—Florescent Infidelity Burner Test. Using a highly tuned infrared lamp, DSI scans for traces of clothing fibers, scent, makeup, and other bodily fluids on the ARSE's person.

Flirtatious Felonies. Provocative conduct, ranging from fleeting flirtations to full-blown encounters, that amply demonstrate how the ARSE's and DUPE's psychographic backgrounds influence romantic, sexual, and emotional potential.

FOCCed UP—Fear of Commitment Compounded by Underlying Pressures. This is often accompanied by a belief that someone better may be out there. FOCCed UP is one of the most common forms of commitment phobias (others include "I'm Just Not Ready Syndrome" and "The It's Not You, It's Me Complex"). Its onset often comes as a surprise, since most suspects will hide their reservations until their fears become so overwhelming, they make a run for it.

GPS—Genital Positioning Sweep. DSI's custom-modification of the Global Positioning System normally used in marine, terrestrial navigation and location based services. DSI uses GPS to confirm reports of infidelity and track genital movement.

HC—Homosexualis Closetus. Homosexual men who engage in heterosexual relationships (ranging from casual dating to marriage and paternity) based on a deliberate or unconscious desire to cloak their gay orientation.

HEAT—Highly Erotic Attractive Traces. Indicates the level of basic attraction and sexual chemistry between parties.

HID—Homosexualis in Denius. Cases in which straight men are assumed to have not yet "discovered" that they are gay.

ICE—Intimate Communications Evaluation. An examination of romantic and sexual interactions to reveal basic compatibility and emotional hurdles.

Interpersonal Infractions. Mild to extreme dating misconduct that causes another person to suffer.

Intimacy Intervention. In lieu of Relationship Rehab, DSI dispatches field agents to assist in the complete removal of an ARSE from a DUPE's life (including all totems and reminders). DSI monitors progress through regular MRI scans of brain patterns.

James Dean Syndrome. Marked by a rebellious streak to strike out on one's own and a concomitant panic of being hemmed in by social/legal obligations. Those afflicted tend to avoid signing leases or buying furniture/real estate, snub planning trips in advance, work in freelance/temp positions rather than 9-to-5 jobs, and fail to RSVP for close family weddings.

John Cheever Syndrome. Marked by long periods of depression, reclusion, or rootless wandering, chemical addiction, and sporadic self-punitive creative expression. Those afflicted tend to spend protracted lengths of time without desire for social contact; view the people who love them with contempt; and believe love, relationships, and all other pursuits are vainglorious exercises of human frailty doomed to failure.

KISS—Kinkiness Indicator and Sensuality Sensor Index. This test is used to gauge an individual or couple's potential for erotic experiment and adventurous play.

LIMP—Latent Intimacy for Males Potential Test. A form of gaydar that assigns a rating to an ARSE's level of sensitivity and "feminized" qualities, utilizing both external physical indicators (aesthetic choices in clothing, interior design, and musical tastes, etc.) and internal emotional readings. The test provides a range of Male Intimacy Potential, from Stuffed Shirt Straight Arrow to Village People Wannabe.

MARS—Male Anti-Relationship Syndrome. A long-term classified study substantiating the idiom that men are, indeed, from Mars. The unearthing of these documents has shed new light on a variety of male dating behaviors once thought to be beyond comprehension.

Mating Misdemeanors. Malfeasant behaviors, ranging from snooping to cheating that impaired the ARSE's and DUPE's previous relationships.

MBU—Missing Boyfriends Unit. DSI's special unit dedicated to tracking misplaced boyfriends, at last bringing closure to these perplexing, unsolved mysteries.

Mistress Madness. Women who labor under the starry-eyed delusion that Mr. Somebody Else's will gracefully ease into Mr. Mine. Often punctuated by a "crisis in rationalization."

MOD—Metrosexualis Over-Dosius. A dating-related disorder whereby a man presumed to be heterosexual displays certain behaviors that, combined with sexual passivity, lead women to accuse him of being gay.

NERD—National Evidence Relationship Database. A confidential tracking system that details the dating histories, psychographic backgrounds, and felonious crimes of those who have reported, or been accused of, crimes of the heart.

NICEASS—Naughty Inter-Cubicle Exchanges Affair Syndrome and Situation. A condition common among coworkers that ranges from engaging in salacious instant messaging to full-out affairs.

OVA—Orgasm Veracity Assessment. Usually administered as part of a SPARK (Sexual Potency and Romantic Kinship) test to specifically track incidents of faked orgasms.

PAWS—Pornography-Addictive Web Syndrome, commonly marked by such symptoms as: A strong interest in pornography (*Jenna Jamesonitis*); an acute inability to distinguish reality from mediated fantasy; an expertise regarding current trends in breast augmentation complimented by strong pre-formulated opinions on which actresses have implants; and a working knowledge of labial pigmentation, genital waxing, and piercings. This disorder, while not an untreatable addiction, has the potential to negatively impact dating and relationships when men use porn as a "short-hand," as it were, for gratifying sexual needs instead of engaging in actual intimate relations with their partners.

PDA—Public Displays of Affection.

PRAT—Past Relationship Assessment Test, which uses magnetic resonance imaging of brain and heartrate patterns to determine an ARSE's true level of interest in another party with whom he has had previous engagements.

RAP—Romantic Attraction Potential. This indicates a couple's full potential for long-term emotional success (rather than merely sexual chemistry).

RDB—Rich Deadly Bore. A man whose physical appearance and social standing draw women like flies only to leave them clamoring for insect repellant.

Relationship Rap Sheet. A report containing the full compendium of an ARSE's or DUPE's past interpersonal infractions, mating misdemeanors, and flirtatious felonies.

Relationship Reconnaissance. An extensive documentation of a couple's history.

Relationship Rehab. A series of specific guidelines issued by DSI to salvage a relationship's potential. Sometimes includes a period of partner-probation.

RIP—Reported Intimacy Priors. A search of the DSI central database to check whether the ARSE or DUPE have reported, or been reported of, previous crimes of the heart.

Robin Hood Syndrome. Marked by a passion to change the world through itinerant grassroots activism requiring them to leave long-term partners for a "higher cause." Those afflicted tend to spend extended periods of time in third world countries; lament how they would "never bring a child into this polluted, overpopulated world"; ascribe more importance to social reform than personal relationships.

SADD—Sexual Attention Deficit Disorder. Egregiously abridging one's sexual desire in lieu of image-based arousal and rote sex scripts, particularly those derived from pornography.

SANE—Self-Aware and Normally Emotional. A test that examines a person's emotional and psychological states to determine their level of emotional awareness and intelligence.

SASS—Sexual Arousal Signal Sampling. Forensic analysis used to determine the level of sexual chemistry and HEAT (Highly Erotic Attractive Traces) between the parties.

SOUR—Sock Odor Undesirable Reading. This occurs when a partner's foul grooming and housekeeping habits negatively impact a mate's ability to experience desire.

SPARK—Sexual Potential And Romantic Kinship. A test administered to a couple to measure the level of sexual chemistry between two people. Often accompanied by an OVA (Orgasm Veracity Assessment).

SPIED—a Suspicious Paranoid Insecure Ex Determination. A test to measure insecurity and distrust based on previous relationships and psychographic background.

STUB—Sex Toys Under the Bed. A test to determine a person's level of sexual awareness and openness by scanning for such things as vibrators, dildos, lubricants, and role-playing garb.

TTA—Trouser Tenting Assessment. Used to determine levels of erectile arousal (or lack thereof) in situations where such is expected.

VPA—Voice Pattern Analysis. When monitoring phone conversations between an ARSE and his/her ex, will use a filter for BTT (Baby Talk Tendencies).

Watercooler Mole. A DSI operative placed within an ARSE's workplace and trained to elicit gossip and relationship chatter.

ACKNOWLEDGMENTS

This book nearly didn't happen. When I first encountered chatter about the possibility of a DSI Unit operating clandestinely on a national level, my inquiries were met with a maze of obfuscation, denial, and flat-out refutation.

But as an ardent toiler in the sex and relationship sector, I refused to back down. I want to first and foremost thank my publisher, Judith Regan, for not only rallying to my defense when a warning to cease and desist came from the Federal Bureau of Intimacy (DSI's governmental sponsor), but for somehow managing to persuade the FBI top brass to get on board with doing a book. Many thanks to my agent, Richard Abate, for helping to convince them that I was indeed the guy for the job. A special thanks to Cassie Jones and Tammi Guthrie for all their editorial insight, as well as enduring a particularly grueling DSI background check, and much gratitude to everyone else on the ReganBooks/HarperCollins team.

I would also like to thank Peter Hyman (author of *The Reluctant Metrosexual: Dispatches from an Almost Hip Life*) and Sue Rosenstock for working with me day and night to assemble the document you now hold in your hands. I couldn't have done it without them. Thanks also to Delia Peretta for coming along for the ride and providing great feedback.

To my extraordinary wife, family, and friends: thank you for putting up with what must have appeared extremely odd behavior and heeding my request not to ask questions regarding this top secret assignment. I'm thrilled we can now return to the joy of our normal lives.

Finally, thanks to all the men and women out there, the ARSEs and the DUPEs, who came along with us on this journey into the heart of darkness that is American dating. From me, and everyone at DSI, we hope you've learned a little something along the way that will keep the mystery of your relationships alive without driving you crazy in the process.